"Every once in awhile, a writer comes along who is comfortable speaking the truth, no matter how much it might challenge us or make us uncomfortable. Naomi Aldort is one of those people. She has a clear-headed understanding of how to empower self-realization for both parents and children.

"Naomi Aldort takes the struggle out of parenting by demonstrating how to replace the controlling and shaping style of parenting with one that values, trusts and nurtures children's innate abilities and autonomy. Simply put, this book is about valuing our children for who they are, rather than for who we want them to be. For many of us, that is not as simple as it sounds, but with Aldort guiding us through our children's ages and stages, it is possible. And that, I believe, is the best gift we can give to both our children and ourselves."

Wendy Priesnitz
Editor of Life Learning magazine, author of *School Free*
and *Challenging Assumptions in Education*

"Insight, resourcefulness, and wisdom are the real subjects of Naomi Aldort's book — qualities vital to joyous parenting. The author is battle-tested in each of these areas and uses a wealth of personal experiences to guide you in finding a successful family formula of your own. Let Dr. Aldort hold your hand for a few hours. You won't regret it."

John Taylor Gatto
Author of *Underground History of American Education*

"Naomi Aldort knows how to raise children who love because they were loved. This book is the antidote to the traditional ways in which almost all of us garden variety neurotics were raised. This powerful book could bring about an end to fundamentalism, moralism and other mental illnesses and social diseases."

Blanton, Ph.D.
Radical Honesty,
founder of and seminars

"In this stunning insight into human nature a window into harmonious family living. Simply and eloquent how parenting can be a path toward self-realization. This book deserves be widely read, and not just by parents but by every being who strives for peace. Dr. Aldort has distilled the essence of peaceful parent-child relationships into what can only be described as poetry of the human heart."

Veronika Robinson
Editor of The Mother magazine, UK

"Naomi Aldort's insight and compassion about living and learning with children can help anyone who wants to become a better parent."

Patrick Farenga
Co-author, *Teach Your Own: The John Holt Book of Homeschooling*

Every parent would happily give up ever scolding, punishing or threatening if she only knew how to ensure that her toddler/child/teen would thrive and act responsibly without such painful measures. *Raising Our Children, Raising Ourselves* is the answer to this universal wish. It is not about gentle ways to control a child, but about a way of being and of understanding a child so she/he can be the best of herself, not because she fears you, but because she wants to, of her own free will.

Raising Our Children, Raising Ourselves

Naomi Aldort, Ph.D.

BOOK PUBLISHERS NETWORK

Book Publishers Network
P.O. Box 2256
Bothell • WA • 98041
Ph • 425-483-3040

10 9 8 7 6 5 4 3
First printing: January, 2006
Second printing: November 2006
Third printing: April 2009

Printed in the United States of America

LCCN 2005936173
ISBN 1-887542-32-9

Editor: Pat Farenga
Proofreaders: Vicki McCown and Lisa Biskup
Cover Design: Laura Zugzda
Interior Layout: Stephanie Martindale
Photograph of Author: Georgi Coquereau

"Nothing you become will disappoint me; I have no preconception that I'd like to see you be or do. I have no desire to foresee you, only to discover you. You cannot disappoint me."

- Mary Haskell

Contents

Gratitude

I started writing this book when my youngest was a toddler, some eight years ago. I was done putting it all in writing within a short time, but was too busy mothering to do any editing and prepare it for print. The book would have been published five years ago, when my youngest, Oliver, was six, but he and his brother, Lennon, decided to take music lessons (cello, violin, piano and later, conducting and composition). Both boys exhibited prodigal talent and so I had to put the book aside for a few more years. Today Lennon Aldort (15) composes and conducts his own symphonies, and Oliver Aldort (11) has been a soloist with numerous orchestras and has appeared on TV and radio; you can see him at www.OliverAldort.com.

The book you are holding in your hands today has been rewritten and transformed many times. In a way, it grew up with me and my three children.

My gratitude starts with my children, my personal coaches and teachers. Jonathan Aldort, taught me, among other things, that no matter how loving and great a mother I may be, the child makes up his own movie of his childhood and this is the only childhood he has. Lennon Aldort taught me to go with a child into his world and discover new realities I didn't know existed. He taught me to distinguish self-deception from deep truth and pointed out to me every time I limited myself with my own thinking. The youngest, Oliver Aldort, is still holding my hand on my way to self-realization, teaching me the Buddha nature. When things don't flow his way he says, "Whatever," and moves on happily. When I torment myself with motherly worry, he asks, "Mom, why are you doing this to yourself?"

My gratitude goes next to the thousands of children who have provided the material for this book. I am at the feet of all the parents who had and have the courage to seek my guidance and share their family stories with me. You will find these stories, with changed names and scenarios, all throughout the book, as well as stories from my own family, with real names (with permission).

My dear husband, Harvey, provided support and resistance; he challenged me, yet always trusted my ability and my wisdom. Harvey is the man who has the courage to seek my guidance with our children. He would call me, saying, "I cannot handle this peacefully with the children. Please do your magic." After I would take care of the situation, he would say, "Get that book out already. The world needs it."

This book could not exist without my mother's ability to raise herself while raising her children and, as a grandmother, by asking questions and always being ready to learn something new. The first person who taught me the concept of validating emotions is my dear mother. She was and remains a progressive and exceptional mother, and is still learning.

I am grateful for the editing and formatting I received from Patrick Farenga, my editor, former editor of the publication, *Growing Without Schooling*, and a leader in the unschooling movement. Pat took my manuscript and brought it to its final shape with grace and a sense of ease. Before bringing the book to Patrick, I was fortunate to work on it with my friend, literature professor, Richard Fadem. He didn't edit my writing; instead, he gave me a crash course in writing and editing.

Thank you Ellen Steiner and Deborah Burke for working with me on the original manuscript. Thank you Lisa Biskup, Michael Biskup, and Chrys Buckley for copy editing the book. My gratitude goes to Victoria McCown for the final proofing and for teaching me grammar. I couldn't finish this book without Sheryn Hara at Book Publishers Network, who took the burden of getting it ready for print off my shoulders. And, thank you to Justin Smith and the staff at Bang Publishing.

I want to thank my friends who read parts of the book and made useful comments: Marjon Riekerk, Kathy Gainor, my brother Kobe Hass and sister-in-law Michele Hass, and others who made useful comments. I cannot possibly mention each person by name, but I am grateful for every morsel of feedback I have received.

The movement toward respectful and natural parenting has been supported by many individuals and organizations. I am especially grateful to Attachment Parenting International and La Leche League, whose many devoted mothers and leaders have distributed my articles and used my work to make a difference with parents of young children. In particular, I acknowledge the mothers of Northwest Attachment Parenting, and other parenting groups in the Northwest and New England.

A special gratitude goes to the many people who have influenced my thinking in their writing. Some are alive and some are gone. Thank you for sharing your thoughts and love: Byron Katie, Werner Erhard, John Holt, Ekhart Tolle, Marshall Rosenberg, Joseph Chilton Pearce, Daniel Greenberg, A.S. Neill, Robert S. Mendelsohn MD, Tine Thevenin, and many others whose words I heard or read without keeping track of who they were. Thank you also to the many people who supported me, wrote blurbs for the cover, and let me know that the book makes a difference: Brad Blanton, John Breeding, John Taylor Gatto, Jan Hunt, Wendy Priesnitz (Canada), and Veronika Robinson (UK).

A special acknowledgment to Peggy O'Mara, editor and publisher of Mothering magazine. Peggy has been a major force behind the movement toward natural ways of parenting. Her leadership has paved the way for me and for others to make a difference in the lives of children and parents around the globe.

Most importantly, I acknowledge you, the reader, for your courage to explore this new paradigm in parenting. Without you this book would not exist. I am a reflection of your commitment to raise yourself along with your children.

With love and appreciation,

Naomi

Preparation
ᴊᵏ

Paradigm Shift

Share life with a child whose competent actions
come not from fear, but from joy and love.

This book is the result of years of mothering and of counseling families from all over the world. What I have learned from parents' amazing stories is that you already know how to be a parent, yet you don't always follow your own wisdom. You might say something or act in ways you wish you hadn't, but the reason you experience regret is because deep inside, you know. Only thoughts and past recordings in your mind get in the way of your wisdom, which springs from your love. In this book you will learn to distinguish unproductive thoughts from your love of your child, so you can act with integrity and be true to who you really are, the loving parent you want to be. You will learn precise techniques to bring out your love in the face of challenging situations.

I know you would happily give up ever scolding, punishing, or threatening if you only knew how to ensure that your child would mature into a kind, responsible, and successful person without such painful measures. *Raising Our Children, Raising Ourselves* is the answer to your wish.

In recent years, a desire for peaceful parenting has brought forth gentler ways of getting children to cooperate. However, the very old concept of control hasn't changed, and "engaging cooperation" has become the new terminology that blinds us from seeing the underlying control. Control is ineffective because humans resist it by their very nature. Whether it is gentle coercion or covert manipulation, the very control we use causes the problems we are trying to solve.

Most parents already know how to control children gently; what we don't know is how NOT to control them and live in peace and joy with them. We know such gentle controls as natural consequences, an agreed-upon "non-punitive" timeout, engaging cooperation, bribes, and praise. Yet, obedience, compliance, and even engaged cooperation mean the child succumbs to the will of the adult, even if she seems content to do so (because she wants your love and she is relieved to earn it). Parents today are looking for ways to raise children without controlling them, while providing nurturing and leadership.

The purpose of this book, therefore, is not to teach you how to elicit cooperation, but how to empower self-realization for both you and your child. *An autonomous child, whose life flows in her direction, acts productively because she wants to. She acts out of joy and love, not out of fear or a need to earn approval.*

In the coming chapters, you will learn how to get your own emotional reactions and conditioning out of the way so your child can be who she is without being held back by your past, by your anxiety about the future, or by your concern about what others may say about you as a parent. You will learn to nurture without shaping, like a gardener who waters the flowers, but doesn't help them open nor choose their shapes or colors.

Our evolutionary progress toward more peaceful, connected, and self-realized human beings depends on letting go of the attachment to the way it used to be and of the need to control. The typical questions: How can I "get her" to do chores, be quiet, stop the tantrum, eat her food, etc., reflect a wish to control the child. It is about "making" the child do what the parent wants; the child has to *give up what she wants, which is giving up on herself.* But, giving up her will is the cause of most of the difficulties with children. It is the child who directs her own life who acts productively, because she acts from joy and love and not from anger, fear, and stress.

If you have the courage to trust your child so that she can direct her own life, you will enjoy the most fulfilling parenting experience, one in which you fall in love with the unique wants and preferences of your child. Such love is unconditional — loving your child, not your idea of how she should be. Love is only love when there are no conditions. The moment love is used as a reward for behavior or achievement, it ceases to be love and instead becomes a lesson in give and take. In this book you will learn to let go of your armor and let love flow through you with no strings attached. Indeed, loving unconditionally is its own reward.

At each tough moment with your child, you have a choice: to stop the child's way of being so you can stay devoted to your old ways or to grow into the greater person you can become by flowing with your child's journey. She is your teacher. Self-directed and self-realized people grow in families where parents are growing up side by side with their children.

Parenting is a path of maturation and growth if we dare to learn more and teach less.

Our quest for control is neither a fault nor a mistake. We are innocently following in our elders' footsteps, which were based in fear. They believed that children don't mature into capable adults unless their parents shape them. They took upon themselves the rather godly role of turning babies and children into adults. Parenting is much simpler when we realize that children come here already designed to bloom in their own unique ways.

In this book you will find great relief from the impossible duty of shaping humans. Nature/God doesn't goof; it is not your job to turn an infant into an adult human over twenty years. It is your responsibility and privilege to care and nurture a human being while she grows.

The coming chapters are based on the realization that thoughts come and go without our control; we didn't put them there. These thoughts are not all useful or even true, and we do not have to obey them. If we want our future as humanity to look different than how it looks now, we need to allow our children to create it out of who they are and not out of who we want them to be. Our aspirations for them are based on thoughts we have inherited from the past. No change can occur by repeating the past and obeying the old fear-based beliefs in our heads.

Dozens of parent-child scenarios appear in this book. They are actual stories of families with whom I had the privilege of working. All names and settings are changed for confidentiality. Principles of love have no relation to age. These anecdotes are from the lives of children of all ages — infants to teenagers.

Parenting is a path of maturation and growth if we dare to learn more and teach less. When you have the courage to stop defending the way you are, or the way your parents raised you, you can open up to the possibility that you are much greater and more magnificent and capable than you thought you were.

Chapter One

꙼

Talk That Heals
and Connects

The words we choose in our interactions with children have
the power to heal or to hurt, to create distance or foster closeness, to shut down feelings or touch the heart and open it, to
foster dependency or to empower. For instance:

> While shopping at a health food store, I heard a
> child crying. I followed the sound and found a girl,
> about four years old, lying on the floor crying and
> whining. No one seemed to be around her. I scanned
> the area quickly and a woman at the counter answered
> my unasked question: "I don't know where her mother
> is. This boy seems to be her brother."
>
> The crying girl's brother was about nine years old.
> He was standing by the shopping cart in the aisle. I sat
> down on the floor next to the crying girl and tried to
> guess why she was crying.
>
> "Have you been waiting and waiting and waiting
> to get out of this store?" I asked.
>
> "Yes," she said.
>
> "Do you want to go home already?"

"Yes," she said, sobbing more fully now.

"This is taking so long, and Mom seems so slow," I added.

"Yes," came the answer. This time the girl looked at me with her big, tearful eyes.

"It's hard to be in this boring store and wait so long," I said.

"Uh-huh."

Her brother then walked over to us and with an impatient gesture said, "Come on, Lizzie, get up now."

I turned to the boy and said, "Are you tired of waiting for Mom, too?"

"Yes," he said, and then he added, "especially when the best TV show is on."

"Oh," I said. "Are you missing your favorite TV show right now?"

"Yes," said Lizzie, and then she told me about the show.

"What a bummer," I validated. "When is this show going to be on again?"

"Tomorrow," they said in unison. "It's on every day," added the boy.

"Are you afraid that you are not going to be able to figure out what you missed?" I asked, thinking they might be concerned about following the plot.

"Yes," said Lizzie, while her brother nodded. Then Lizzie got up. I introduced myself. Lizzie gave me a warm hug. I said, "I'm so glad I met you." She sank into my arms and I stood up holding her. She was calm. Then her brother moved closer and said, "I'm sure we'll figure out what we missed on the show, Lizzie." Lizzie smiled.

At that moment the children's mother came over and thanked me for my help.

Talk that heals doesn't necessarily change anything. Lizzie didn't get to go home when she wanted to and she still missed her TV program. What changed is how she felt about it and how she spent the rest of the time in the store. The more common way of talking often negates every pronouncement of the child. Let's look at how the conversation with Lizzie would have looked like if I "lovingly and gently" negated her.

Suppose I had asked Lizzie, as she lay on the floor sobbing, "Why are you crying?" Asking "why" puts a child on the defensive and implies that we don't see a reason for crying; whereas, as a general rule, children believe that the reason for their tears should be obvious. "Why?" can also infer a damaging accusation to a crying child: "Something must be wrong with you to be so upset over that." For the purposes of this example though, let's imagine that Lizzie had responded to my question, "Why are you crying?" with "I want to go home."

"I'm sure Mom won't be long," I could have said. "Want to see something?"

At first glance, this last exchange may appear harmless, yet it denies Lizzie's feelings not once, but twice. First, to Lizzie, Mom is taking a long time to finish shopping. By inferring otherwise, I would have contradicted Lizzie's sense of impatience. Second, by offering to distract Lizzie from her distress, I would have implied, "Let's pretend you are not feeling upset and let's make believe you are having fun." This negates her need to be present to her emotions and her desire to speak about her upset and her wishes.

If Lizzie falls for the diversion, she may stop crying briefly. Yet, because her distress is still acute and her feelings remain denied, the diversion, no matter how appealing, will not take care of her emotional needs.

For the story's sake, let's say Lizzie doesn't fall for my attempt to distract her and cries all the more loudly, "I want to watch my TV show. I want to go home now!"

"I'm sure you can watch the show another day," I might have negated some more. "Besides, too much TV isn't good for you."

At this point I would have alienated Lizzie to such an extent that she would have wanted to escape. I would have minimized her sense of impatience, dismissed her feelings of frustration, attempted to distract her from her real feelings, and inferred that she had no cause to be upset. Therefore, it would have been unlikely that Lizzie would have persisted with her striving to express her feelings or ask for what she needed because she would not have perceived me as being on her side.

My talk with Lizzie could have gone on indefinitely because negating never resolves anything, but rather escalates painful emotions because the child is driven to defend her story. Eventually she would have found a way to rid herself of me, feeling more upset than she felt before.

When children perceive that it's okay for them to be authentic, that it is fine to feel what they feel, and when they see that we care about their point of view, they will often create the solution to their problem, or make peace with reality. In contrast, when children's feelings are negated and denied, they are often unable to resolve their problems. They feel angry because they perceive themselves as victims.

In the pretend scenario, I would have alienated Lizzie to such a degree that she would have been bound to transfer her righteous anger to her mother, further escalating her own and her mother's distress. On the other hand, what actually happened in my presence is that Lizzie felt relief when validated. She could then accept that she would not be able to watch her favorite television program.

Does Validation Work?

"I validated and it didn't work," said Annie with a desperate sigh.

"Did you want validation to stop your daughter's temper tantrum, and it didn't?" I asked.

"Yes," Annie said, "and she still didn't put her blocks away."

Validating is its own result. It is not a method we use to control or change the course of a child's upset or behavior. On the contrary, validation and focused listening are our way of making it safe for the child to express herself; it is our way of offering love and intimate friendship. The result of such validation is that the child feels safe to feel her feelings and to express herself fully.

The most likely immediate outcome of validation is more crying, a tantrum, or other forms of self-expression. In the real scenario with Lizzie, when I validated her feelings, she responded by sobbing more fully, giving vent to her upset. Only after she was done crying and talking about her needs did she become calm and able to face reality. When such validation comes from the child's parent rather than a stranger, the child is likely to cry for a longer time, releasing old stresses together with the immediate ones. Children whose feelings and experiences are validated may cry more or they may become angrier precisely because your validation gives them permission to express their deepest feelings. Once they are done, however, they often move on with no residue of bad feelings.

Sometimes validation does bring an upset to a quick end because the issue is temporary, so the child feels a quick relief. However, if the child increases her sobs, be there for her. Be sure you are not causing the anguish, but providing love and validation for a needed release. If you become uncomfortable with the intensity of emotions, remind yourself that your commitment is not to your own comfort, but to your child's sense of trust in you and in herself. Through such self-awareness, children come to know and to trust themselves; emotions and their expression, including intense ones, seem less scary to them.

Not only does the child grasp her own emotions and needs clearly, but in validating your child's feelings, you will also find that you understand her and that both of you feel deeply connected and empowered. You will develop respect for her individual journey, as well as a clearer grasp of your own parenting path. A deep bond of trust will grow between you and your child, which she will carry on to other relationships for the rest of her life. In trusting herself and having no fear of feelings, she will have emotional resilience and compassion with which to face life's ups and downs.

When validating feelings, avoid dramatizing or adding your own emotional reaction. When we dramatize, the child is likely to dive deeper into her story; if she experiences our benign attitude, she can cry or rage fully and then see her own "drama" and laugh about it or at least move on with a positive outlook.

Lizzie and her brother found their own peace in the face of reality because they were fully heard and at the same time their story did not gain momentum. I avoided dramatizing. I did not evaluate the situation, nor did I offer ways out, which would imply that the situation is bad. Children jump right out of their misery when validated with a benign attitude and when they are done expressing themselves.

Communication S.A.L.V.E.

Many parents ask for precise words that will help them change from negating to validating and empowering. The S.A.L.V.E. formula can be a tool to help you in making the shift toward affirming your child's experiences so he can let emotions be and act authentically and powerfully.

S - Separate yourself from your child's behavior and emotions with a Silent Self-talk. This is the hardest step; once you can do it, the rest flows easily. Notice that when your child's action elicits your reaction, your mind puts words into your mouth. It is like a computer running itself: Your child does something and a window opens automatically inside your mind. This would be harmless if you didn't read what it says out loud. If you are upset, it is the wrong thing to say or do and will only aggravate the situation. It is not what you want to say. It does not represent your true intention and is therefore inauthentic. The proof to this inauthenticity is that later you regret your words and actions and they build walls between you and your child.

To avoid hurting your child, read the words on the automatic window silently in your head. Notice the words you almost spoke and let your full expression occur inside your head, including visuals, actions you want to take, or memories from your past. This takes less than a minute and it harms no one. Whatever you feel is yours only and not a reason for action or utterance. It is an old record and it is not who you are in the present.

Initially, this investigating of your own thoughts may need more time than the one minute. Start by just noticing and letting your thoughts be. Write your thoughts down so you can work with them more thoroughly later. With time you will gain greater control over your mind and you will be able to run the whole little process on the spot.

Thought investigation:

- Check the validity of the words that drive your upset, anger, worry, or criticism. Are these really *your* words? Do you really believe them? Thoughts like "She will never learn," "He shouldn't behave like this," or "She should know to take responsibility" are old records you may not even agree with. Maybe they are what others say; maybe they are your fears, your memories, or what you aspire to for yourself. One way or another they stand in the way of your ability to love and understand your child the way she is.
- Notice what these thoughts do to you when you take them seriously. Observe in your mind *how you treat your child when you obey the thought.*
- Consider who you would be if the thought didn't cross your mind. Without the thought, you can be free to respond to

your child rather than to your own mind talk. Try to imagine facing the same situation with your child, only without the thought that drives you to negate and control. The thought will not vanish. It is yours to keep. Just imagine who you are without it. Without your limiting thought, your real, unconditional loving self may emerge.

- Check and see if what your mind says about your child isn't just as true about yourself. We usually see in others things we need to hear for our own sake. "He shouldn't behave like this" becomes "I shouldn't behave like this...with my child." "She will never learn" can also be a call for you to look at your pace of learning to be a parent, and "She should know to take responsibility" can be the greatest guide for your own ability to be responsible for your mind's reactions as well as other components of your life.

Once you become aware of the thoughts that mislead you, you will discover that who you really are is unconditional love; instead of being caught in your own anxiety about the child, you will be present with him with nothing but your love as it always was and is. With the clutter of thoughts removed, the light of who you really are shines right through and your child is seen in that loving light.

A - Attention on your child. When you have silently investigated the conversation inside your head (which has nothing to do with your child), shift your attention from yourself and your inner monologue to your child.

L - Listen to what your child is saying or to what his actions may be indicating; then listen some more. Make eye contact with your child and ask questions that would provide him with an opportunity to speak some more, or if the child expresses himself non-verbally, to let him know that you understand.

V - Validate your child's feelings and the needs he expresses without dramatizing and without adding your own perception. Listening and Validating are the ingredients of love (LV). When you succeed, you create a connection with your child and you feel present and authentic with yourself.

E - Empower your child to resolve his own upset by getting out of his way and trusting him. Show confidence in his resourcefulness by not getting all wound up and by not rushing to fix everything. Children come up with their own requests, solutions, and ideas when feeling able, trusted, and free of parental expectations or emotions. Feelings get in the way of the ability to act powerfully. Once these feelings are expressed, the child regains his freedom and focus and will either let go of the need or come up with solutions. In a quick and natural way, he will be doing what you did in your self-investigation.

> *Nine-year-old Clint was crying because his sister Joy wouldn't finish playing Monopoly® with him. "I want to finish the game. I was so close to winning!" he cried.*
>
> *Ella, their mother, was ready to enforce "justice," but she took time to separate her personal reaction from her children's dispute and run her own self-talk silently in her mind (S of S.A.L.V.E.). She imagined herself yelling at Joy, calling her inconsiderate and unkind, and ordering her to finish the game. Then she examined the thoughts in her head and was clear that it was not the truth; her daughter is not unkind at all and her ability to assert herself is a good thing. She*

was then able to let the thought be and move on to giving (A) Attention to Clint and (L) Listen to him.

"So you were very excited because you had a chance to win. Are you disappointed that you didn't get to finish the game?"

"I am mad. I want to finish the game," Clint insisted.

"I hear that you want to finish the game and Joy won't play."

"I was so close to winning and that's why she stopped," Clint said.

Ella kept Validating and Listening, but not changing reality for Clint. She empowered him by not getting involved in fixing his reality, as though she were saying, "I hear you, I don't see a problem, and I know you can handle it."

After a while he was done and started a different conversation.

Clint was heard. He felt connected to his mother who had validated his feelings and repeated the facts based on his perception. She did not add drama; she did not mix in her own emotions or opinions. Her trust and consistent presence made it possible for Clint to move on.

Young Children and Emotional Words

Talking about feeling sad, upset, or disappointed may or may not be grasped by a younger child. Instead, young children feel most validated when facts are acknowledged. In a phone session, a mother told me about her experience with her daughter at the pool.

Orna (5) came out of the swimming pool, crying desperately because she wanted to stay longer. The swimming pool was closing for the day. Her mother,

Donna, dressed her to get out of the building. As she was dressing Orna, Donna validated her child's experience by stating what was so:
"You love to play in the water. Did you want to play much longer?"
Orna responded with "Yes, I want to jump more."
Donna continued, "I know. You didn't want to get out of the water yet, and we were told to leave."
Orna stopped crying and said, "I love the pool."
"Yes," said Mom, "and you don't like to be taken out of the pool."
"Mom," responded a calm Orna, "I don't mind any more. I want to go home."

Donna described the facts only and Orna could easily relate and feel content with her mom. On their own, children do not cling to painful emotions. They move on powerfully because they don't have a load of history around each feeling. Avoid teaching them the adult art of "wallowing in one's misery." Adults sometimes go on and on trying to generate guilt in the other person, or even to blame the culture or the government. I am sure you don't want to teach such skills to your child. Validate, yet expect her to move on; expect her not to take her emotions too seriously and learn from her. Emotions are a form of discharge, just like sweat and a bowel movement. Emotions need to be acknowledged so they don't get in the way, just like sweat has to be washed off. Once the child's need for understanding is met, she will move on. Her ability to move on will also prevent her from clinging to the event and turning it into a story that could negatively affect her attitude for the rest of her life.

When Validation Becomes an Insult

Sometimes validation can negate a child's sense of privacy and autonomy. A child can perceive your caring words as an insult when her upset is about something you have done or said; a child may also resent validation regardless of the causes for her upset. She needs the freedom to choose whether to expose her feelings or not. She may not want the fact that she is upset to be mentioned. In essence, the child is saying, "When I am upset, let me be, but don't tell me that you see me." When a child has such a need for silent listening, any word we say is most likely to embarrass her.

> *Five-year-old Amber builds a tower. The tower falls and she becomes upset. Her grandma comes into the room and validates, "Oh, are you frustrated? Do you wish it didn't fall?"*
>
> *Amber pushes the rest of the standing blocks and screams, "Don't say anything!!!"*
>
> *Grandma sits there quietly, realizing her mistake.*
>
> *Amber then throws herself on the floor and pushes the blocks around angrily. She yells, "Stupid blocks, stupid floor, stupid me!" She throws more blocks all over the room. Grandma is silent but present, and Amber responds to her attention by being fully expressive. When she is done she gets up, picks up the blocks, and calmly builds a tower.*

Silence does not mean indifference. Give full attention, just don't mention it. It is also uncomfortable for a child to have her feelings mentioned when she is embarrassed or scared. In such instances you can either say nothing and stay attentive or reassure a child by exposing your own humanity as you tell her of a similarly embarrassing event in your life, as my client Adi did:

> *While Adi worked in the yard, his four-year-old daughter, Ruthi, went inside and poured herself a glass of milk. Some of the milk spilled on the table and the kitchen floor. When Adi came into the house and saw the spilled milk, he was ready to burst out with, "Why didn't you ask me to help you? You know you can't do this by yourself." Instead he took a deep breath; he noticed these words pass by silently in his head (S of S.A.L.V.E.) and that they were not useful to him. He then turned his attention (A) to Ruthi. He realized that she had been trying not to disrupt his work and was pouring herself a glass of milk without his help. He came closer and said cheerfully, "I see you had some milk all by yourself."*
>
> *Ruthi responded, "Yes, and some of it spilled." She looked up at her father with a questioning look.*
>
> *"That happened to me the other day at Grandpa's," he said. "I spilled juice. I felt clumsy, but Grandpa smiled and gave me a towel. It's easy to clean up."*
>
> *Ruthi ran from the kitchen and brought a towel, which she handed to her father. It was not the kind of towel Adi would have used to clean up the floor, yet he accepted the towel with a smile and cleaned up the milk.*

By recognizing and acknowledging Ruthi's achievement of pouring herself a glass of milk, Adi treated her in the same way he would have treated a guest who accidentally spilled milk. In admitting his own clumsy moment, Adi provided validation without putting Ruthi on the spot with words that expose her emotions. Recognizing that even her father is clumsy sometimes, she felt at ease. When she brought the "wrong" towel, Adi did not criticize her nor did he change the towel. In this example, spilled milk created a deeper bond between father and daughter, and the child's self-esteem and dignity stayed intact.

Angry Feelings, Loving Words

Sometimes, in spite of all our intentions to love and be kind, what we might feel toward a child is anger and even resentment. The trigger does not have to be big. Each one of us has her or his memories of pain and shame that surface when confronted with even remotely similar situations.

We don't necessarily recall anything, but the emotions associated with those experiences flood our mind. The S.A.L.V.E. formula (Separate yourself, Attention on the child, Listen, Validate, Empower) can be used with special emphasis on the first step.

Anger and violent reactions tend to cover up other painful feelings. These are often feelings that we may not be aware of because of fear and discomfort rooted in our past experiences. If, when you were a child, it was not safe to feel sad, to cry, to request attention, and to express yourself fully, you are likely to have suppressed these emotions long ago. What occurs in the present is automatic; the painful feelings get "filed" away instantly and anger puts itself in the front because it is more acceptable and you feel less vulnerable than when you show your sadness or your tears.

Yet, anger does not give us the release we need because it focuses on blame. Putting our attention outside of ourselves (blame) prevents us from feeling our more vulnerable emotions.

Unless we investigate the thoughts that cause our anger, we stay incomplete and often angrier and more attached to this painful victim (blaming) position.

Think before you act or say anything in response to an unexpected behavior of your child (Self-talk). Don't say the first words that come to your mind. These are the words that will, most likely, hurt your child and escalate the struggle; although these words won't vanish, you will learn to see them as thoughts, not as truth. You can even get your child's help with this process. Ask him to remind you to "Take your time, Mom" or "Think for a minute, Dad." You can give your toddler a "flag" to wave at you as a reminder. Those agreed-upon key reminders can signal you to take a "time-out" for yourself so you can separate your inner conversation from your child's issue and from your authentic self. Attend to your emotions first and you can generate freedom to be focused on the child.

The child is the stimulus, not the cause of your anger; he is not responsible for your emotions. He took action and an old program opens up on your mind computer and demands that you do what it says. You have no choice over this automatic response; however, you can choose to obey it or not. You can be your own inner listener and let out the steam internally so you can attend to the child, free of these old reactions. If by taking a little time to Separate yourself you have come to realize that the thoughts that feed your anger are not really who you are and do not relate to the present, you may be able to simply notice them, let them be, and put your full attention on the child. Later you may want to find a listener, a friend, or a counselor to complete your own investigation of your thoughts. You can also do it by yourself. Write down each anger-producing thought and check its validity for you, how it makes you feel, and behave, and how you would respond without it. Then find out if much of your expectation or judgment of your child may be just as useful for your own growth.

Be kind to yourself. The key is not to make any judgments about your thoughts or fantasies; they are not an authentic expression of who you are and of the parent you wish to be. Take about a minute or so and express yourself fully, only inside your head. You can fantasize yourself yelling, hitting, blaming, threatening, punishing, and whatever else your mind may come up with. Run your inner "movie" to its completion and to your satisfaction and then ask yourself if it is really relevant to the present and true to who you are. You will be so happy that you didn't follow up on these movies.

When you give yourself the freedom and love to let it all flow freely in your head, it takes very little time but gives you back your power and your love. You are just observing your thoughts and looking at the contents of your anger. If you can take another minute, put these thoughts in writing and check their validity for the moment. After working through this "truth process," you will feel much more able to focus on the present and on your child's innocent intention. A mother who took my advice relayed to me the following story:

> *While Wendy took a nap, nine-year-old Emory decided to surprise her by preparing the lasagna dish they had planned to take to a potluck party that evening. When Wendy woke up and came into the kitchen to prepare the lasagna, she found Emory, covered with*

tomato sauce and standing in the middle of a tomato puddle, with tofu and cheese scattered all over the countertop. A baking tray was filled with ingredients that wanted very much to look like lasagna, but looked to her more like mashed potatoes in tomato soup.

Wendy was ready to explode. She didn't have time before the party to clean up the mess and make another lasagna. She took a deep breath to start S.A.L.V.E. She saw herself yelling and cursing, yanking Emory out of the kitchen, and forbidding him from going to the party. After the angry words and fantasies passed through her mind unspoken, she put her attention on Emory. Before she had a chance to say anything, Emory said, "Mom, I made the lasagna. We only need to bake it and clean up. You can go back and sleep some more."

Now aware of her child's loving intention, Wendy smiled and said, "Thank you. What a surprise. I feel refreshed. Can I help you with the clean-up?"

Emory accepted his mom's help. Wendy noticed that the lasagna did not look as bad as it appeared to her when she was angry. Emory was proud of himself and Wendy learned a valuable lesson. Mother and son had a wonderful evening together.

Not only was Wendy able to shift her attention and see her son's action with delight, by being silent she also made it possible for him to initiate the first words which resolved everything. Often, when upset, we jump to conclusions without finding out the facts and the intention behind the child's actions. Waiting until a child initiates communication can take the wind out of the sail of anger and bring clarity to the situation.

Being masterful and loving in testy moments is easier if we remember that it takes just as much time to clean up a child's mess when we are angry as it does when we are delighted with him. When we spare the child the words that trigger guilt, resentment, and shame, he feels worthy, cherished, and appreciated. It is those connecting emotions that make our time with children worthwhile for them and for us.

Making Requests of Your Child

There are times when we wish to ask a child for something we need, to hang the towel up after a shower, to end a phone call, to move the noise to another room, or to take muddy boots off before entering the house. The words we choose in these situations can blame and shame a child or they can generate consideration and mutual care. Until recently, blame and shame were tools of control, which did not generate care but induced compliance by fear. Typical phrases like "How many times do I have to tell you?"; "What's wrong with you?"; "You have ruined everything!"; "If you don't...you are going to get it!" are still ringing in many people's minds from their youth.

Sometimes the control was more subtle and we felt obligated without knowing why, as when parents said, "Jamie is such a good girl; I know she will help you." We were praised for meeting our parents' needs and ignored when we didn't. We were told that loving our parents meant doing what they say. We were bribed with food, praise, love, privileges, or gifts, and we were manipulated through a variety of coercive measures. These ways of getting compliance were no less controlling, only more covert. Children who were controlled in these manners were often feeling confused by what seemed so gentle and loving yet left them feeling small, shamed, and inauthentic.

After generations of growing up doing out of fear what parents say, we are finally embarking on treating children with
the same dignity we wish for ourselves. Putting to final rest the
old concept of expecting a child to do what a parent says does
not come easy. It requires commitment and consistent practice
and self-control. You may find it most helpful to take a minute
before asking your child to do something and to ask yourself,
"How would I (or would I) make this request of an adult friend?"

In the new paradigm children are not obligated to meet our
needs. They are free to generate their own choices and responses
to our requests, and we do best when we honor their choices and
when we are considerate of their limitations and their aspirations. Our task is to communicate with children, as we would do
with our adult friends, without inferring that we expect them to
do as we ask. If our request is not granted, we need to either
accept it respectfully, or show our understanding of the child's
preference and discuss possibilities for meeting everyone's needs
or find a solution that both the child and we can be happy with.

Make your requests authentic; don't pretend to do something for the child's sake when it is for your sake. For example,
it is you who needs the room clean, not the child. You want to
teach, but the child does not want to learn. Premature teaching
is like premature birth, it has a price; it slows down the learning process and puts a wall of mistrust between you and your
child. Trust your child's developmental stages, and make your
requests honest, "*I need* the room clean." Your child may or may
not help you clean, but he will learn about your aspiration for
order and will eventually want the same for himself (or find
someone to live with who will, which is fine, too).

Grant your child innocence and think twice before making any request. If your toddler comes in the house with muddy shoes and walks across the carpet, she has no awareness of any problem. You can simply state the facts: "Your shoes have mud on them. Let me take them off you." Then clean the carpet.

When we start cleaning the carpet, a toddler may or may not choose to help. It does not matter if she participates in the cleaning. Coercing or insisting that she help will only lead to feelings of failure, resentment, and guilt. These painful feelings prevent the development of an authentic desire to be helpful. On the other hand, watching us clean while feeling good about herself, or leaving happily and finding it clean later, allows the child to absorb our ways and eventually choose freely to participate with us. If your toddler offers to help, allow her to assist you without criticizing, helping, or cleaning up after her in her presence. You may invite her to bring the broom or help, but avoid managing her, so she can make her own choice to participate, to watch, or to leave.

When reprimanded, young children are often too scared by a parent's intense emotions and judgment to be able to even grasp the nature of what is being communicated. Even a slightly harsh tone of voice with the right words, or a covert blame in the sweetest of voices, are too overwhelming for the emotions of a young one and take her attention away from noticing what is at hand. She is too busy feeling hurt or scared. It is when the child feels the flow of life and love unhindered and her dignity unharmed that she can best become aware of the many habits and needs of her fellow humans. She does not need help in learning to live with us; she needs us to trust her and not to get in the way of her learning.

If you only use the S of S.A.L.V.E., the rest will come naturally. Once you investigate your mental chatter or let it pass without obeying it, you can be present with your child rather than with your reactions. Whether making a request or responding to an upset, as soon as you are present and free to give attention, you are likely to connect with your child and to know what to do.

Rewind

"S.A.L.V.E. works when I remember to do it," said a doubtful father. "But what if I don't remember to take my time? What if I just burst out with anger?"

Indeed, changing habits is not easy and you will fall back on old patterns of behavior. To transform yourself from a habitual "negater" to a "validator" you need time and practice. Begin by noticing your negating comments without trying to change them. Don't mentally berate yourself because you have negated your child or spouse. Developing kindness starts with being gentle and patient with yourself. Investigate it after the event. It is only a voice in your head. Watch it go by and you will gain a moment in the present. Investigate its relevance to the moment and you will gain clarity. Sense how you would be without it, then look at how what you expect of your child may apply to you, and you will be moved to love yourself and your child.

With regular practice, you'll gradually learn to stop your mind in mid-sentence and change direction. When this occurs, you may be able to acknowledge your error to your child, "rewind," and start over.

We can learn to take advantage of replaying unsatisfying scenes as in theatrical rehearsals. You can even say to your child, "Rewind! I am going to redo that last scene." With practice, you will catch yourself in time to let the negating words go unuttered and turn to your child with a listening heart and an open mind. For instance, a father who attended one of my workshops rewound his arrival home.

> *Norm entered the house and found a huge mess of broken cardboard boxes and smashed crayons all over the floor. He started complaining about the mess and demanding that the children clean it up immediately. The youngest of the children, Miranda, started to cry while her older brother Leon said, "But, Dad, we are in a middle of a game."*
>
> *"This is not a game, destroying all these boxes and crayons," Norm yelled...and then, abruptly, he stopped his yelling and said, "Rewind! Let me do this scene over."*
>
> *Theatrically, Norm walked backward and left the house. He then reentered with a smile on his face: "Hi, children, how is your day going?" He kissed each child and his wife and continued, "Oh look at this, what are you creating here?" The children hurried to explain their game as love and interest were restored.*

It takes time and practice to master such awareness. After all, we have all grown in a culture where negating is automatic, a culture that taught us to identify with the automatic words of our mind. We negate so unthinkingly that it does not even represent what we really think or feel; we are not being authentic. Yet, it won't help you if you start judging yourself for having such human thoughts. You are raising *you* too; be kind to yourself. Start by making a simple guiding agreement with yourself: When upset, do not say the first words that come to your mind; those are bound to negate and to hurt someone. You can "rewind" as soon as you catch yourself, even if you are deep into the scene or at its end. It is never too late to wake up from a nightmare.

Catching the negating conversation inside your head is the building block for transforming yourself into a validating and kind communicator. It may take you a few months of just succeeding to catch your negating talk once in a while, but eventually it will replace the old habit of losing control and of having your old movies run your life.

If you have ever practiced a new language, musical instrument, or other difficult skill, you know that it takes time and repetition to master anything. Practice does not make perfect; practice makes permanent. Your old habits got a lot of practice over many years. Let your child know "I am new at this. I am learning."

Validating Unspoken Communication

There are daily opportunities to validate a cranky, aggressive, or sullen child who is reluctant to share his feelings in words. In a counseling session, a mother, Rebecca, told me about her success in connecting with her child.

> *Rebecca noticed that her son, Josh, was grumpy after school and said, "I wonder what it is like for you. I remember when I was in the fifth grade. I hated my teacher and I didn't have any friends. It was such a painful year for me." Josh perked up, asked some questions,*

and then said, "The teacher scolded me today and then Rob and Dan made faces at me and didn't play with me at recess."

Rebecca was careful not to inquire about the reason for the scolding and not to name emotions. Instead she kept validating his experience in neutral mode: "Gee, what a bummer." Josh could tell that his mother understood him so he continued, "I hate that teacher. Whatever I do is not good enough for him."

"You did what you could and he still scolded and criticized?" asked Rebecca.

"Yes," Josh responded, "and when he does that, my friends laugh at me. I hate school."

Rebecca sat down next to Josh and put a loving hand on his shoulder. Her touch brought Josh closer to his feelings. Tears streamed down his cheeks as he related to his mother more details of his experience and a few other stories of agony from school as well as from his relationship with his sister. He felt much better afterwards, and mother and son were closer to each other and ready to embark on productive solutions.

In the next couple of months the family explored the possibility for Josh to home school. Josh wanted to stay in school that year but the following year he chose to direct his own learning outside of school.

It helps children to know that their parents have also experienced rejection, loneliness, fear, and failure. One father started sharing memories from his childhood with his son. In about a week, the boy started opening up.

Children always communicate, even when they don't use words. Some children will act out their fears in imaginary games. Or their fears may present themselves as an increase in sibling rivalry, bed-wetting, an inability to concentrate, or a tendency to be grumpy or aggressive. Other children respond by shutting down their emotions, retreating to their room, and spending time lost in painful conclusions. It is easier to overlook the fact that they may have just as intense emotions as a cranky sibling who expresses himself by whining, hitting, or crying.

Both the child who acts out and the child who shuts down need to express their feelings in order not to be stuck in them. When stuck with unexpressed emotions, the mind tends to inflate the story into a drama that often hinders emotional freedom for a lifetime. (Notice that any area in which you feel scared or otherwise limited, you have a story about it from your past.) In later chapters you will learn how to provide your child with productive opportunities to unleash feelings of helplessness and other distress. This chapter focuses on ways to create a connection and bring ease to talking about painful emotions.

Communicating About Losses

When unchangeable events occur (death, divorce, or illness), open communication is the most important aspect of recovery. When a child is lonely in her inner world, the impact is long-lasting and painful because she will identify with the pain and make her life story out of it. She needs to know that she is right to feel what she feels and to have the fantasies she has; by expressing these feelings she will also discover that they are not her identity. She will then be able to distinguish her true self from the thought process that causes her pain.

There is no need to protect a child from unavoidable hurts, but you do need to be in communication about her experiences.

A mother told me she planned to inform her three-year-old daughter that her cat died only after she could get her daughter a new cat. Following a session with me, she changed her plan and told her daughter about the cat's death that day. She listened to her child's feelings and was surprised when the girl did not care to have another cat.

Find time to talk about new realities every day. Share memories, and let your child know that crying, remembering, and speaking about feelings is a normal and healthy way to deal with intense pain. When a child or a toddler expresses her anguish through play, physical displays, or art, make sure to receive and validate the communication. However, it is important not to add drama to the child's expression, so she can freely choose to move on when she is ready.

How to Express Regret So the Child Will Feel Healed

A child, like an adult, cannot feel satisfied with "I am sorry." To be complete, she wants you to show that you know exactly what occurred for her, such as, "You were playing in the water and they were closing the pool. You refused to leave and I took you out of the water." After she tells you her side of the experience, ask her how she would like you to handle such a situation next time.

Sometimes parents apologize even when there is nothing to apologize for. They may say, "I am sorry, but you can't have that candy." To the child it seems that if Dad were really "sorry," as in "sad," he wouldn't persist with forbidding the candy. Indeed, the child will be glad to relieve you of your "sorrow" and get the treat. Such dishonest messages lead to confusion; in contrast, being authentic will provide clarity for your child. Instead of telling her what she can or cannot have, which sounds controlling and negating, speak in a personal language that expresses your choice: "I don't want you to eat this candy because it is unhealthy." When our communication is clear it is easier for a child to flow with it or to make a clear request: "Can I get one that's healthy?"

We want to acknowledge regretful actions or words, but when we say, "I am sorry I hurt you," we take responsibility for the child's emotions. Although we may regret what we did, and realize how we have triggered pain, we must grant the child the dignified right to be the only author of her own feelings. In addition, when we imply that we caused her feelings, we insinuate that she is weak and not in charge of her own reactions. She then learns to experience herself as a victim and to blame others for her emotions.

Obviously, your child has little control over her reactions, yet she is the source of how she feels and acts. When we speak in a way that acknowledges her ownership of her feelings, she will develop emotional resilience and will have more choice and control over her reactions.

To avoid planting feelings in your child, let her initiate her responses.

A mother told me how dismayed she was with her son's response to what she thought was a devastating calamity. The boy's father trashed the child's computer document, saying, "It wasn't marked." He knew it was his son's and that it was a story the child was

composing. He felt angry to find an untitled docu-
ment and thought that trashing it would teach his
son a lesson.

Upon finding his story gone the boy expressed dis-
may at his father but was not angry. His mother felt
enraged and asked, "Don't you wish your dad would
at least apologize?"

The boy was calm. "No, it doesn't matter. I will
write it again and it will be better."

"But aren't you furious?" she persisted.

"I was for a second," the boy said. "But then I
realized that it was useless to be mad as it won't change
anything, so I thought it is actually good."

The next day the father said, "I made a mistake
trashing your document. In the future, I will not trash
anything without asking first."

The boy was satisfied.

When you realize your words or actions have elicited intense feelings in your child and you want to undo the hurt, acknowledge what happened and find out what she feels. Speak simply and directly: "I yelled at you. I wish I hadn't." Avoid exaggerated emotional words so she has freedom to be authentic. Stay attentive, and let her find what is true for her. If she talks, listen and validate, but don't dramatize. If she is not yet verbal, she may show you how she feels by playing it out with a doll, acting, drawing, or just sitting in your lap quietly. When she is done you can express your own feeling simply: "I feel sad because I want our relationship to be one of appreciation and respect." Then make a plan for a better future and let her know about it.

When you avoid taking responsibility for a child's feelings, you might make the common mistake of saying, "I am sorry you feel bad about it." This phrase can come to mean that you did no wrong and it is only the child who responded with the "wrong" feeling. The result is usually rage. Stick to describing what occurred and your child will be able to trust you and to know that you care about her, not just about erasing the record of your regretful behavior.

Sometimes it may seem to you that you are really and absolutely right and have nothing to acknowledge. However, your child's upset is the evidence that there is a need for communication. You don't regret plucking her out of the street, but if she felt startled, you can restore the trust between you by acknowledging your swift action and by listening to what she has to say about her experience.

Cleaning up our errors is not a trial; it is not about being right or wrong. If your child feels hurt, her feeling is her real experience. If you regret your words or actions, your feelings are valid as well. Your goal is to generate a connection between the two of you, gain clarity, and rebuild the bridge of trust.

> *Five-year-old Jessie came to his mom, crying. He said that his brother, David, who is twelve, broke his Lego® car. Jessie couldn't put the car back together and David refused to repair it. Linda came into their room and scolded David who ended up sulking.*
>
> *When Linda called me she said that she was right and she has nothing to apologize for. However, after considering David's hurt feelings, Linda realized that there were better ways to express her feelings and that she wanted to connect with David and to find out what was going on for him.*
>
> *At the next session she told me about her conversation with David.*

LINDA: *David, I had a session with Naomi about what happened yesterday and I realized that I wish I would have been aware of your needs. Could you tell me how you felt when I scolded you?*

DAVID: *Oh, nothing.*

LINDA: *Were you feeling frustrated when I accused you of being careless and all that?*

DAVID: *Maybe. But it doesn't matter now.*

LINDA: *I agree. I waited too long. But I do want you to know that I regret the words I used and I wish that I would have found out what your experience was.*

DAVID: *Yeah, yeah.*

LINDA: *I sense that you don't trust that I really care.*

DAVID: *You don't.*

LINDA *thought for a minute, then continued: I feel sad because it is very important to me that you are heard.*

DAVID *was silent.*

LINDA: *Would you be willing to help me understand how you felt?*

DAVID: *Okay.*

LINDA: *When Jessie came to me crying, were you feeling outraged?*

DAVID: *Yeah, very. He is such a crybaby and he never tells what he did. You always fall for his whining.*

LINDA: *So you felt angry and you wished that I had found out what really happened?*

DAVID: *Yes, or just not intervene. Jessie took some Lego® blocks from my spaceship to build the truck he was playing with. I asked him to give them back and I said I would build him another truck from some other Lego® blocks.*

LINDA: *David, I can see now how furious you must have felt when I took sides with Jessie and judged you without even knowing what happened.*

I feel relieved that you told me all of this. I think next time I will just validate Jessie's feelings and let you two solve your problem.
DAVID: *That would be good, Mom.*
LINDA: *And if you guys need help resolving a dispute, I will listen to each one of you and help you come to a solution. Will you be willing to remind me if I forget?*
DAVID: *Well, I don't like to, but okay.*
LINDA: *I will do my best to remember on my own.*

If all Linda had said was, "I am sorry about scolding you yesterday about the Lego® blocks," David wouldn't have believed her, and rightfully so. He would have felt even more furious. "She thinks if she says 'I am sorry,' it erases what she did. Well, it doesn't...she always protects him..." and so on, adding chapters to his evolving life story about not being loved as much as his brother. Instead of an apology, the completion that Linda initiated brought son and mom to a place of understanding and a loving connection, and David's drama is dissolved.

Some parents expect an "apology" from a child and judge when it is not forthcoming or not said in "the right way." *Always be the master of yourself only,* grow in kindness, and learn to cherish your child wherever she is in her ability, readiness, and development. When you know that your child may be harboring a sense of guilt and does not dare to connect with you about it, you can relieve her of the burden by bringing the subject up and resolving it. "Do you feel uncomfortable about the lost key?" Listen and then let her know, "I will make another key and I am sure the old one will show up eventually. I lose things too. It can happen to anyone." A hug and other loving expression will ease her tension and resolve it.

When Communication Tools Backfire

Sometimes it seems as though we are being validating and attentive, and yet a child seems only put off by our words. There are a few possible errors we can make that lead to a child's resentment and isolation in spite of our validation and care. We cannot cling to rigid formulas; we must develop sensitivity to the child's nature and an acute sense of respect and delight with who he is moment by moment.

The human tendency to turn any idea into a tool of control is something we need to constantly guard against. Any communication approach can be turned into a device of control. We can use validation to gain control; we can manipulate by using it; we can even be disrespectful while using these skills of communication and trigger a child's rage. Children sense when we manipulate them even when they can't clearly explain their discomfort.

If you don't even know how your words drive your child away from you, keep in mind that people are insulted when they sense that another person has control over their feelings and behavior. They want to defend their autonomy. Keep the child's dignity intact by having no intentions for him to be any specific way. Communicate kindly for your own sake, expecting nothing in return, so the child can be free to feel and be, in his own way. He may express rage or burst out with laughter. He may be peaceful or distraught. He may express himself or he may not. When you don't have a goal other than to connect with your child, and when you don't judge his choice of expression, you are less likely to patronize and control and more likely to be authentic and kind.

The first common error is insulting a child by stating (instead of asking about) his feelings: A child mopes around the house and you say, "You must feel upset that your best friend is away for the summer." You may be correct, but the urge to forecast a feeling can be perceived as patronizing.

Instead, you could give feedback and ask a question: "Can I ask you something about yourself?" If the response is positive, and if the child awaits your initiative, you can ask a question based on your observation: "I have noticed you walking silently back and forth. Is there something that is bothering you? Would you like to talk about it?" Children need to know that their inner world, their thoughts and feelings, are not the targets of comment by their parents. You can make it safe for him to share his heart, yet it is up to the child to speak.

If a child wants to share his loneliness with you, his sadness, or any issue he may have, he will do so if he knows that you care and that you will listen and validate his feelings without advice or criticism. Feeling safe in your presence, he may eventually talk to you about what is bothering him. You can make yourself available by showing interest and offering your ears: "I can spend time with you and listen after dinner."

If this approach is new to you, and your child has already been harboring hard, unexpressed feelings for a while, you may need the help of a counselor to heal the relationship. Feelings of hurt and anger that are harbored and have no outlet hinder the emotional, intellectual and physical well-being of the child. You can also help yourself get closer to your child by doing a daily process of investigating your own disturbing thoughts. Write them down and go through the S part of

S.A.L.V.E. Check the validity or relevance of the thought in the face of reality; notice how you feel and act when you obey this thought. Imagine yourself without this thought, in the same scenario and listen to your own teaching as it applies to you. When, through this investigation, you discover the errors you have made, you have a chance to apologize and make amends, which will rebuild the trust between you and your child.

Another obstacle is our tendency to think that we know what is good for the child. We need to trust children completely and assume that when they see themselves as worthy, loved, powerful, and free to express their feelings and thoughts, they will take care of themselves and communicate their needs optimally. If we treat children as we would treat adults, we will be less likely to think we know what they need. We show a friend kindness without expecting him to change for us, and we don't talk to a friend with the goal of controlling him.

We would do well to treat children with dignity, respecting their limitations and aligning ourselves with their authentic self-initiated goals. We can listen to their feelings while empowering them to act free of their constraints. For example, when feeling scared to audition, your child needs to express himself so he can then have the freedom to do the audition. When you listen to his fears and doubts, don't join his feelings; instead, hold him in your mind as auditioning. You are the clearing for his emotions so he can move on powerfully in spite of his concerns or choose not to audition freely and not due to fear.

As you develop your communication skills, avoid the tendency to judge the communication abilities of others. You may be tempted to criticize your spouse, friend, or child for not communicating "the right way." Parents especially tend to evaluate each other and their children by complaining about their lack of kindness or by accusing, "You aren't validating," "You're not expressing a feeling," "You are judging," or "That's negating!"

Words of judgment separate us from those we love. Teach no one but yourself. When your spouse, relative, or child is judging or demeaning, express yourself authentically by letting him know how you feel or by guessing his unexpressed feelings. For example, when a child says about a sibling, "She is such a liar," you can ask him a validating question like "Would you like to tell what you know about what happened?"

When you must disapprove of an unacceptable action, no judgment is needed either. Speak personally about yourself, not in slogans about right and wrong. For instance, saying "It is wrong to steal" is not likely to evoke remorse; instead, a child will feel shame and alienation. On the other hand, when you say, "When I found out that you took candy from the store without paying, I felt sad and worried," your vulnerable words are likely to touch and inspire your teen to talk about what drives his desperate actions.

Many people worry that this approach will strip them of the right to defend moral thoughts. On the contrary, you get to express your values more potently when you do so with personal words. When pointing fingers and waving rights and wrongs in the face of the accused, we only lose him; he cannot hear us. When being vulnerable with your personal experience, your child, spouse, or friend will not feel threatened or alienated, but connected and moved by your communication.

An introduction to the five primary needs of children

Understanding Your Child's Behavior

"There is no right or wrong behavior. The only meaningful choice is between fear and love."
- Gerald Jampolsky, Ph.D

Parents often call me because they are bewildered by their children's behavior. They want to respond kindly but find themselves unable to do so. Many parents already know the way to communicate kindly, but they say that they can't get themselves to use what they know.

It is our own mind-talk that prevents us from understanding the child and from knowing how to respond. A child's actions are not bad or good; they are simply expressions of emotional and physical needs or they are innocent play. Yet, our mind quickly evaluates a child's actions, and we respond not to the child, but to our own interpretations of her actions.

Responding to a clear request for physical needs like sleep, food, or warmth seems easy. However, when the child's needs are emotional or when she expresses herself in ways that collide with our preferences, we may experience reactions that range from confusion and anger to helplessness and despair. These reactions are not authentic in the sense that they are old thoughts and not a direct response to the child; they prevent us from seeing the child clearly as she is in the present. These thoughts are rooted in our past and get projected into the future, usually as fears about the child's development or about our image as parents.

In other words, we often misunderstand a child because we are too busy listening to the automatic reaction inside our head. The mind plays old records, and as human beings, we are designed to identify with that inner voice. We obey the voice that plays automatically in our head even though it is not in harmony with whom we wish to be and who we really are.

Responding with wisdom and love occurs when we are completely present and free of old mind chatter. Love can only be experienced in the present. If you could be present with your child you would not need this or any other book. It is only our mind that sends complicated messages. For example, a toddler may pull a toy out of her baby sibling's hand. The parent may hear her own mind saying that this is cruel or rude, but the toddler is acting innocently on her own behalf. She is either being playful, she needs that toy and does not yet recognize the baby's humanity, or she may like the baby's reaction or want your attention. When you notice your child without labeling or analyzing, you can respond effectively and peacefully, as illustrated through many examples in the coming five chapters.

When a child's actions provoke your annoyance, anger or pain, you might be tempted to eliminate the behavior. Yet, this does not work and even if the behavior is eliminated (through fear), another will show up in its place to represent the same unmet need. Your child is your teacher; when you get rid of the lesson by stopping her, both of you lose. If, instead, you investigate those thoughts that cause you to negate her, as you have learned in Chapter One, you will grow in emotional freedom and you will be able to respond, rather than react, to your child. Realizing that the child is expressing a need can help us shift our purpose so it is no longer about stopping the child's expression, but about finding what he needs. When we stop the child's expression, we stay stuck in our old hurts and we don't understand him. In contrast, when we distinguish our reactive thoughts as old records and investigate them for validity and relevance, we can learn how our mind works, and we can then see the child with clarity in the present.

In other words, it can be said that the greatest obstacle to our ability to understand the child is that we take our own reactive thoughts and opinions to be truths or as useful guidance. As you read the following chapters, you will learn a few ways to distinguish your loving guidance (focused on the child) from your reactions (focused on you). One clear distinction shows up in the result: Loving guidance leads to peaceful solutions and heartfelt connections with your child, while in contrast, reactions lead to struggle, anger, and disconnection.

Often the actions a child takes are the actual fulfillment of his needs, as when he needs to run around endlessly, imitate the hauler monkey with screeches, or turn the bathroom into a tropical rain forest. Understanding his intent makes it easy to either let him be or provide an outlet that won't interfere with your own preferences or with the well-being of others. What gets in the way of loving and of understanding the child's expressions is our mind's chatter about fear of losing control, of the child not developing well, or of other mind-created dramas and expectations.

Once you focus on your child, you will find it easier to respond kindly. The five basic emotional needs that drive a child's behavioral language are:

- Love
- Freedom of Self-Expression
- Autonomy and Power
- Emotional Safety
- Self-Esteem

When consistently fulfilled, these basic experiences form sturdy foundation upon which children can exercise their potential and live powerfully and contentedly with themselves and with others. In other words, a child who feels secure in parental love, one who feels worthy, autonomous, and safe to be and to express herself fully, will thrive and stay connected with herself and with you. On the other hand, children display behavioral, learning, and other difficulties and disorders when they are feeling emotionally unsafe, helpless, lonely, or insecure.

The following chapters provide insight into the many behaviors with which teens, children, toddlers, and babies communicate these five basic needs and enriching ways to respond to them.

Chapter Two

༺

Love

We don't water a flower if it blooms;
we water it so it will bloom.

Loving a child does not guarantee that he will experience him-self as being loved. When a child is not aware of the love we feel toward him, he may feel insecure, unable to express him-self, or helpless. He may resort to destructive behaviors or he could become compliant and suppress his authentic self as a way to gain our approval. The reasons for not feeling connected to us can be that we do not express love in a way that the child perceives it, that he experiences himself as secondary to a sib-ling, or that the love is given conditionally.

We don't water a flower if it blooms; we water it so it will bloom. Likewise, a child needs to feel secure in our love so he can flourish. By contrast, when love is used to control the child, he ends up doubting it. For example, if your father expressed love to you only when you behaved a certain way or brought home good grades, you may have wondered deep inside if he really loved *you*. A child is not here to be evaluated and then rewarded with love. Every child is born worthy and deserving of love. Love is only love when it is unconditional.

Sometimes parents confuse being loving with letting a child do whatever he wants. No one gets to do whatever they want all the time. For instance, we don't get to drive as we wish; sometimes we stop when we want to keep going. There are considerations for the needs of others that limit our freedom as well as protect it. This has nothing to do with love. Bending the world to fit a child's every whim can hinder the natural development of his emotional resilience. The child is born into a real world and into your social community. He wants to belong and be part of the real social web of family and friends. Treat him as your equal while being considerate of his limitations. He may not have the ability to wait or to share yet, but that does not mean that he can trash your house, get every toy, or pull your hair. Loving him, therefore, is finding considerate ways to meet his needs and being empathic and empowering when life does not provide for his every desire.

The other side of loving your child on his terms is accepting his unique expression of love as well. A child needs his expression of love to be received even if we have to be inconvenienced. We may get annoyed when a child makes a big puddle on the bathroom floor, yet, he may be cleaning up as a way of expressing his love to you. Keep Winnie The Pooh in mind when you think your child is being destructive: Eeyore's house looked to Pooh like a pile of wood, which he then took apart in order to build a house for Eeyor.

Both receiving and giving love must be unconditional. If a child has to measure up to be loved and if he needs to weigh his own expressions carefully, he becomes anxious and doubtful of his own worth. Indeed, such striving for love becomes a rat race to please or live up to expectations, a race in which a person never feels satisfied because he feels unworthy at all times other than when he proves himself right or pleases someone. This is the essence of low self-esteem. We feel insecure when we fear that our performance or behavior might not bring the acceptance we so yearn for. An intense desire to measure up is the result of seeing ourselves as not measuring up and of feeling loved only when we do.

It is not that our parents did not feel love toward us, but that for many, freedom to express love unconditionally was hindered by cultural norms and by the unresolved pain from their own upbringing. Many of them didn't experience unconditional love even though their parents loved them absolutely. When facing their own children, these parents may have felt painfully unable to give that which they did not experience. Indeed, many of us grew up fearing that if we didn't do as our parents expected, they wouldn't love us, a feeling we don't want to pass on to our children. Instead, let us adopt the attitude expressed by Mary Haskell in a love letter to the poet Kahlil Gibran: *"Nothing you become will disappoint me; I have no preconception that I'd like to see you be or do. I have no desire to foresee you, only to discover you. You cannot disappoint me."*[1]

When a child has no doubt about your love and admiration of him, his contentment is the ground on which he can succeed in his endeavors. He will be able to act on his own behalf authentically, free of worry about eliciting your approval, and when he wants to please you, he will do something that meets your need (not his own need for accomplishment); he will not help nor be considerate to earn your love, but because he loves you.

To understand how to ensure that the child experiences being loved, we need to avoid using love as a commodity to give or to withhold in exchange for a behavior or an accomplishment. Love is the context in which you hold the child so he can feel free to be himself. His choices and behavior do not affect the context of love, and solutions to difficulties are found within that context.

Loving your child is seeing his magnificence and finding value in his point of view. It is not that you love the mess he made or how he hurt his sister, but when you come to these situations from love, in the here and now (not replaying your old records), you see his need and you say, "Oh, what fun, spreading the beans all over the table," or "I see how upset you are with your sister. Will you show me (tell me) how you feel?" as you gently get him away from his sibling and assist him in finding productive solutions to his dilemma. You love his choices and direction simply because of loving him, which helps you tune into his being and offer solutions. Quieting your mind and being present will help you access your own wisdom and love. Observe what your mind is saying; investigate it as outlined in Chapter One, then move into the present with your child.

Love Is Not a Reward

Parents are often puzzled by the idea of expressing love toward the child who acts aggressively; yet, when you do, you will discover that your child's aggression is her cry for your love or for your attention to some unmet need. Your love is therefore the best answer to her distress. She has no control over the way her feelings pour out (similarly to an adult who yells or says hurtful words).

The aggressive child does not perceive herself as being rewarded by your love. Instead she feels relieved because she is understood and cared for, which will help her resolve her anguish. By stopping her act and offering your love and care, you give your child tools for kind and peaceful relating. When children feel secure in parental love, they are hard to provoke into hurting another.

We love the child, not her achievements or behavior. Love is a context that colors everything. If we feel upset with a child, all we need to do is "apply" love and we will find ourselves delighted with her (even if we must deny her choice). To be able to do so, you must investigate your thoughts (S of S.A.L.V.E.) so you can be present. Your thoughts are not you. They come and go without your having any control over them. They are not the truth; if you grew up elsewhere, you would have had different thoughts. Find out if these ideas enhance or hinder your love. Further in the chapter you will find examples of observing the thoughts that get in the way of love.

You know you love your child; therefore, if your words or actions aren't kind and loving, you are not being true to your-self. When you find solutions within the context of love, they are peaceful solutions that honor everybody's needs and dig-nity. The old belief about tough love is just another thought that justifies hurting a child. With exception in those rare instances where safety of the child is paramount, and you need to intervene forcefully (pulling them quickly out of the road), love doesn't hurt, it loves.

If we were unconditionally cherished when we were children, we would need no guidance on how to love. We would then have no other way known to us other than loving our children abundantly and with no relation to their actions. It is our personal pain and fear that gets in the way of letting go and of loving unconditionally.

Our experience of scarcity is one of the reasons we are afraid to give. We may fear that the child will take our love for granted and will take advantage of us. We may feel vulnerable in giving abundantly. This is the same fear that may have stopped your parents from expressing their love to you unconditionally. (Overcoming these and other obstacles to loving will be discussed later in this chapter.) Yet, the child is best off taking your love for granted. Such a healthy assumption about being loved is the ground on which a child thrives and grows into a compassionate, loving, and capable adult. Instead of wasting her energy trying to gain approval, she is free to engage in accomplishment and growth.

How Children Experience Love

The following are a few guidelines to keep love flowing and to have it be recognized by your child.

Meet Needs

When a child feels safe to express himself, when he has power to steer his life and he is secure in knowing that his needs are taken care of, he can experience himself as worthy and loved. Therefore, the first avenue to ensure that your child feels your love for him is to trust him and to meet his needs on his terms. Unmet needs translate into perceiving oneself as being unworthy of love and suffering the painful emotional consequences of such a perception.

One way a child expresses his needs is by making requests. A baby uses crying and other physical cues; the toddler lets us know of his needs with behaviors and with words. Meet your young child's requests with a readiness to interrupt your activity. Be prepared to say "Yes" and to do what it takes to supply his aspirations and meet his needs. The dishes can wait; his soul cannot. The phone call can be postponed; love cannot. A new dish can replace the broken one; broken souls become scarred. A mess can be cleaned and damage repaired; your child's sense that you love him is derived from his noticing that he is more important than things and schedules.

Responding promptly to needs does not mean that you can never count on a child to be able to wait for you to complete something. As he gets older, and when he feels secure in your love for him, he will gradually become capable of accommodating some of your needs too. Trust the process so that it comes authentically from him. Let the initiative be his, so you know that he does not act to earn your love. Don't expect consideration for your needs prematurely because, when sensing your expectation, he may live up to that to get your approval, and we are back to conditional love and manipulation. Indeed, children are prompted by expectations to do what would please the adults around them, which hurts their sense of trust and self-esteem.

Protect the child's authenticity in his relationship with you so when he is considerate, it is because he cares and loves you. Acting out of a need to get your approval, rather than from an authentic desire, leaves a child feeling resentful and unsure of your love. These negative feelings will actually hinder the authentic development of his desire to care for others.

You may wonder then about the common belief that high expectations prompt high achievement. Indeed, within an academic or skill-building endeavor, the standards set by a teacher with whom the child has freely chosen to study can support the student's pursuit of excellence. A teacher and a student are equal as people, but not equal on the training court. The student has chosen to take the teacher's guidance and often pays her to set up expectations that will further his quest for learning.

Such expectations have no place in a loving relationship between parent and child (or any love relationship) and they harm both the relationship and the authentic development of the expected trait. You have not been hired by your child to direct his life; but instead, you have volunteered to respond to his needs and to nurture his growth with love.

Expecting a child to develop at a pace set by you contradicts loving him for who he is, because his worth is then measured by your standards and timetable. Instead, loving your child is being delighted with his pace of growth so that he feels free to be himself at each step of the way, free of the concern that you won't love or appreciate him if he doesn't live by your time-table or standards.

Stay present to the love that you have for your child. Instead of expecting respectful behavior, treat your child with respect; instead of expecting him to be able to wait and be considerate of your needs, be kind and generous with him. He will emulate these qualities over time because he loves you and he wants to belong. This does not mean that you can never ask him for anything, but stay within his likely capacity. You can ask him sometimes to be quiet, to wait, or to bring something, but respect his choice whether it is a "yes" or a "no." He will eventually learn to honor people's preferences as well as his own.

As explained earlier, love and responsiveness do not mean giving the child license to do harm or freedom to do whatever he wants (which no one has). It means that you are responsible to provide for the child and to honor him, so he can grow up at his own pace.

Letting go of our vision for a child's behavior and achievements can be difficult. When the baby is born, we automatically envision that he will be an "easy" and "good" child who will grow up in our positive image of kindness and success. Looking at the culture around us, we get caught in the timetable of expectations; he should be doing chores by a certain age, say "please" and "thank you," be responsible, clean, and quiet. You must have noticed that sometimes you even measure your own worth by your child's behavior, especially in public. Is he measuring up? Am I a good parent?

In a phone counseling session, Amanda's mother, Kara, spoke to me about her embarrassment with her daughter and by investigating her thoughts, she came back to adore her child as she is:

> *Amanda was a sweet little baby, easy, smiling a lot and willing to go anywhere and fit in quietly.*
>
> "*I was sure she would develop to be a cooperative, bright girl. Now she is seven, and since age three or so, I hardly ever go with her to visit other people and children because I feel so embarrassed. She used to push and grab. Now she bosses other children around and doesn't clean up after herself. When she comes in, it is like a tornado sweeping through the house.*"
>
> *To assist Kara in investigating the thoughts that obstructed her vision of her daughter, I said, "Tell me more about what your expectations are."*
>
> "*I want her to notice the mess she is making, clean it up, and play with children as an equal,*" *Kara said.*
>
> "*Do you think she can be the girl you envision her to be?*" *I asked. (This is the part where she finds out if her thinking is relevant or valid.)*
>
> *Kara sighed, "No, she is not that kind of person right now."*
>
> *I stayed silent and Kara thought about her own simple insight.*
>
> "*I love Amanda so much. But, I guess, I love her the way I wish for her to be, not the way she is.*" *Kara broke into tears. "I want to love her the way she is and I can't."*
>
> "*What's in the way is only your own thought. Can you imagine yourself with her, without the expectations that she should be neat and relate as an equal?*"
>
> "*Yes, oh yes, I would just love her as she is. I do love her so much.*"
>
> "*What are you afraid you would lose if you delighted in these qualities of hers?*"

"*People will think I am a bad mother because I don't control her.*" (*This is another painful thought that Kara has discovered.*) "*Oh, that's terrible. I keep her from having a social life so I can look good. How awful.*" Kara was sobbing.

"*Yes,*" I said. "*Can you see how your expectations of her could be your own lesson and how it would help with Amanda if you listened to your own instructions?*"

"*I don't know. I want her to clean up her messes. I guess I need to clean up my own messy mind about her. I also have plenty of physical messes to clean up.*"

"*What about your wish that she would behave as an equal?*"

"*Oh, of course, I would love to treat her like an equal. I don't.*"

"*And,*" I added, "*treat yourself as an equal with other parents and people. You don't have to be better than anyone with some angelic perfect daughter.*"

"*Yes, I can see that.*" Kara said and started to laugh. "*It is all about me. You know, sometimes I do succeed to just let her be. Every time we go to the playground, she is so happy and active. She also loves tumbling, and she can play with water colors and play dough for hours. I suppose she can also enjoy baking. But, what about bossing children around?*"

"*What about it?*" I asked. "*Is your thought that she shouldn't be bossy useful or relevant?*"

"*No. She is bossy. If I didn't have the thought that she shouldn't be bossy, I would admire her leadership. I am so scared of it because I am such a shy person myself.*"

"*So, Amanda is one who takes charge. She is responsible for the bigger picture. We need leaders. You have a great teacher.*"

At the end of the session, Amanda and her father (Kara's husband) showed up at the door. Kara sprang *out of her seat and hugged Amanda for a long time, tears running down her cheeks. "I never knew how much I really love you, Amanda. I love you because you are you."*

In the coming weeks Kara watched her daughter's leadership and provided her with opportunities to create safe messes, to build, to tumble, to swim, to jump on a trampoline and other outlets for her exuberance.

"I thought this would be so hard," Kara said, "but, not only do I adore who Amanda is, but most of the problems we had vanished. She even wants to clean up her paint and play dough messes once in a while because they are hers and she can't use them again if they dry in disarray. She is happy with herself and with me.

"The most amazing thing occurred in a visit with her cousins in their house. When Uncle Dave came in and said to put the toys back in place, Amanda told the girls what to do and, under her leadership, the toys got put away peacefully."

Kara did not have to give up the values that she had been passing on to her daughter. On the contrary, she expanded them to include the value of flowing with another on her path. Amanda will learn to include the preferences of others because her own direction is respected. Children want to succeed in being part of this society. They absorb values of love and consideration by benefiting from them first. Trust your child; he will let you know when he is ready to accommodate some of your needs and he will go in and out of doing so in the process of developing partnership.

Physical Affection

Those of us who received plenty of hugs, cuddles, and kisses as children tend to be naturally affectionate. Yet, if you didn't get enough physical affection as a child, you may need to consciously bring yourself to receiving and giving it. Children need all types of affection every day; however, it is the physical expression of love that is the subject matter in this section. Kisses at bedtime, hugs, or a cuddle on the couch can all nurture the soul, as long as your child's acceptance and enjoyment of them are clear. Many children don't like kisses, but will "purr" when you cuddle with them.

For a child who rejects physical affection, you may need to find a mode of body contact he will enjoy. Some children avoid hugs and kisses. These children are often in the greatest need of touch but they feel too vulnerable in their physical need and are often very sensitive. If your child is one who displays discomfort around touching, provide physical affection that is less direct — drawing on the back with fingers, eye-to-eye contact, an occasional gentle touch, cuddling to read a book, and other touchy activities. In addition, sleep with your child or spend bedtime next to her; much cuddling, personal conversation, and love can be shared while she is falling asleep. Co-sleeping can cure and prevent many emotional maladies for humans of all ages, so don't hesitate to follow one of nature's greatest instinctual guides of cuddling to sleep with your child.

Keep giving affection to your teenager. She needs it badly, but doesn't dare to ask. Boys often don't get enough affection as teens. Don't fear his size and sometimes his cool demeanor.

He too needs affection. Don't touch him in front of friends or in public, but do offer a hug, kisses, a massage or, if he will let you, an arm around his shoulders while watching a movie or reading together.

Children who tend to express stress with aggression are often those who also don't like much parental touch. This may be the result of feeling guilty and undeserving, or it may be part of their sensitive nature. Obviously, affection can help this kind of child in her struggle to feel secure in your love and therefore become less aggressive. A child who resists touch may also be physically sensitive; she may need you to adjust the amount of pressure to avoid feeling tickled or she may prefer only back rubs for a while. Use opportunities like bath and bedtime to care for your child's body with tender touch. In addition it would benefit a child to witness parents being physically affectionate with each other and touching in kind ways.

Some children develop an aversion to touching because they may be getting affection they don't want. It is crucial to respect a child's body. Grandpa may think that a kiss for good-bye is an important ritual, but if your child does not want a kiss, her dignity has to be honored. Physical affection is to be shared on the child's terms. Parents have no "rights" to their children's bodies. Demanding a hug, insisting on lifting, or kissing are not affectionate acts because they violate the child's body. While obviously you enjoy hugging and touching your child, make sure that you satisfy her need and do not exceed it. Your respect of your child's body is also the best protection from any physical misconduct that she may encounter.

When we treat the child's body with dignity, she will benefit from the affection. Such affection builds self-esteem, stimulates good feelings and intelligence, reduces anger and violent emotions, develops a healthy and fluid body, and helps the development of closeness and caring.

Giving Attention

Although they rarely verbalize it, children wonder, "Am I important enough for my parents to spend as much time with me as I need?" Children don't seem to feel connected by love if you give them only your partial attention. A child may insist that you look at him when he tells you something, and if you glance away, even for a second, he may pull on your chin to bring your focus back. He may then start his story over. If you play a game with him while reading, being on the phone, or falling asleep, he does not get his dose of love. Likewise a child cannot have a sense of loving connection when he has to share it with a sibling. Even sharing attention with a friend does not replace focused personal time.

Some parents worry that they will "spoil" the child by making him the center of attention. However, focused attention is different from revolving life around the child. It is about a bond of love, similar to what we do with our spouses and friends. Can you imagine a friendship or a romance without focused one-on-one time? Humans thrive emotionally and intellectually on such closeness.

If, in addition to the family, you wish to expand the circle of relationships for your child in a way similar to the tribe or extended family, you will need to provide such a community. Your child will be able to relate to many individuals and create strong bonds with some of them. Yet, he still derives much of his self-perception from relating to you intimately on a daily basis.

To enhance your child's experience of being loved, give him uninterrupted one-on-one time when he is your only focus, and spend that time following his lead. He needs to experience himself as important in your world and see you are eager to put aside reading, house- or paperwork, errands, phone calls and visits with friends to spend time with him. If you have more than one child, this will require some planning. On the other hand, when you are your child's only companion much of the day, focused time with him not only spells out your love, but meets his basic need for human closeness. Indeed, when you are your child's only companion, refusing to be close with him can result in self-doubt and low self-esteem. Giving attention is the loudest pronouncement of love when it is focused and given one-on-one.

Teenagers, like toddlers and children, need one-on-one attention. They sway between proving they don't need you anymore and testing whether you are still there for them. Respect your teen's need to shape his life autonomously, but don't fail the "test." Join him in his conversation with interest; learn about his life, his thoughts, and his feelings, and offer support, participation, and your joy in sharing life with him. Mostly listen to what he has to say and put full attention on whatever he wants to show you or share with you. It is very important to him that you really see him for who he is and that you love how he is turning out.

After he has his cup of attention filled, your younger child may feel content as your companion while you cook dinner, pay the bills, or practice your music. When his need for attention is fulfilled, even a young child can gradually become able to be without it for short and random duration. Let this development show up; don't try to cause it nor expect it.

> *Dawn had a hard time visiting and serving her guest Sarah while, at the same time, responding to her dissatisfied toddler, Dona. Dawn called me that evening in despair, saying that she hadn't seen Sarah for years and needed her child to let her enjoy the visit. In the session, she discovered that her thoughts, "My guest and I should be able to visit without any interruption" and "My guest, Sarah, needs full attention all the time," were the cause of her stress.*
>
> *After the session Dawn made new plans: The next morning, instead of repeatedly telling Dona to wait, she asked her guest to wait or join her while she spent a couple of hours giving her child full attention. Sarah became part of the joyful morning because Dona wanted both of them to watch her dance, sing, and jump. After a couple of hours Dona had had enough and started playing by herself. She was so content that Dawn and Sarah could talk the rest of the morning with hardly any interruptions at all. In the afternoon, Dad took Dona for a walk after which another half an hour of giving complete attention allowed them to visit till dinnertime.*

It is fulfilling the need, not starving it, that leads to the child's ability to move on and away from that need. On the first day, when Dona's need was not met, the day ended up all about her (child-centered) and no one was satisfied. In contrast, when her need for attention was met, she was content and life did not revolve around her. This is also true long term: The more you respond to your young child's dependency, the more independent he will become as an older child and as an adult.

Provide both full attention and shared experiences. If you only provide focused attention, you will deprive your child of the opportunity to create himself as an individual and to engage himself independently. Your child will give you clear cues as to his need for either, attention and for engaging himself on his own.

Shared times can include doing your work with your child by your side. He is then included in your life in a setting of your choice. Avoid working side by side longer than your child can handle. Be sensitive to his timing so that the experience is a positive one. If you want him to join you on your choice of activity, make sure he freely chooses to watch you or to follow your guidance. A child's ability to be part of others' projects will gradually grow as a result of his feeling fulfilled and satisfied with each experience; he will also grow into it easily when he can count on getting full attention when he needs it and when the activity fulfills some of his own interests.

When giving attention, a child will not feel connected by love if you use your time together to get him to do what you think he should be doing. In such cases, he will most likely experience himself as a vehicle for meeting your needs and he will try to live up to your expectations. While doing so he is likely to feel rather anxious about himself and doubtful of your love. When, instead, you follow his lead, he will feel a bond of love with you and he will also develop the ability to initiate activities and establish his own interests.

> *Max didn't seem as happy with himself as he used to be and his mother Leanne became aware of how much he actually rejected her ways of expressing love, especially verbal ones. In fact, he didn't want her to express love with words at all. Leanne began paying close attention to how Max perceived being loved. She discovered that he wanted her to listen to his endless talks about wooden dinosaur kits, which were the center of his life at the time. The tip-off came one morning when Leanne saw how hurt he looked in response to his older sister's annoyance at all this carrying on about dinosaurs.*
>
> *When Leanne gave Max her full attention and listened to his excited talk about the measurements, appearance, and stability of those wooden creatures, his face beamed. To bathe in his mother's love, Max needed her to give him focused attention and to be interested in the things that were most important to him. She went on to be with him in this manner every morning. As his self-confidence in her love returned, so did his natural exuberance and joy.*

Sometimes we think we are following the child's lead, yet we try to sneak in a little teaching or guidance. This too takes away from giving attention as a five-year-old taught his mother at my family counseling retreat:

> *Jeremy was learning to ride a scooter. He asked his mother to sit outside and watch him. As she watched him struggling with his balance, she made a suggestion about the placement of his foot.*
>
> *Jeremy stopped riding, looked at his mom and said, "I asked you to watch me, not to teach me."*

Giving attention is the heart of loving. It requires a complete acceptance of the child, following his direction and responding to his ways of connecting.

Perceptions of Love

What your child needs is defined by her alone. She will feel connected to you when you transmit your "I love you" messages on her wavelength, not yours. If she likes to play outside a lot, loving her is providing a safe yard and sharing outdoor experiences with her. If your teenager wants to be with friends and wear goofy clothes, loving her means making her social encounters possible. If your toddler is a climber, your loving action is to provide her with climbing opportunities; if she likes to cuddle, she will benefit from an affectionate afternoon on the couch or a piggyback ride.

When you get your own agenda out of the way, you stand a good chance of being able to sense your child's reality and notice her individual mode of receiving love. She will feel secure when you take action that resonates with her perception of being loved. Unlike the words "I love you," with which many parents casually, and at times haphazardly, express love, an authentic expression of love must spring from an interaction in the present. Your child may feel nourished by a story, being held, or being listened to. You can tell her how much you enjoy being with her, how much you cherish this moment of being together, or how enriched you are by getting to know her. Most of the time your expressions of love do not convey as much love as does your meeting her needs on her terms.

Similarly, loving your child does not mean buying her gifts every time you are in a store or working extra hours to provide her with designer clothes. Although we perceive ourselves as purchasing such items out of love, our children often do not experience love by receiving these gifts. Instead, your child may miss your loving presence when you are too busy working and shopping. She may also perceive your excessive gift giving as an easy way to appease her without really spending time with her. Gifts can express love when a child's choice is in mind, and when delivered with an authentic expression of appreciation and closeness.

Pay special attention to actions that may contradict your expression of love. For example, a child who perceives love primarily through touch and hugging may feel confused when you tell her that you love her, while she watches you holding the baby. The best way to ensure that your child is absorbing your love is by expressing it in her way, with actions that validate who she is and show your sincere joy in her existence.

On Being Child-Centered

Some parents are concerned that by giving one-on-one attention they are being "child-centered," and they think that this may impede the child's social development. These parents wish that a child would experience himself as part of a community and not as its center. They often look to the tribe or the extended family for the model that gives the child a sense of being a part of a greater social existence. Yet, idealizing the tribe only blinds us to what is available to children in our time and culture.

The nuclear family is not a tribe and does not provide a greater community experience; it does, however, provide a sense of belonging. In a family, a sense of belonging and of becoming a contributing family member grows from caring for each family member as an individual and from one-on-one relationships. Life need not revolve around one child in the family, yet he can receive personal attention. This child is not the only one who gets personal attention; he experiences himself as part of the family and learns to care for the needs of others. Each family member is equally valued. Giving attention is like feeding and nurturing; it is a response to a human need. The child learns his own value by being worthy of our time and attention. He also learns the value of himself and of others, by watching you caring for yourself and for others; if you are worthy, so is he.

Many parents yearn to provide a community similar to the tribe for their child because they like the fact that a child is engaged with other people and children and his need for communal activity and companionship is met abundantly. If you value such an upbringing, by all means create it for your family by joining or starting a co-housing or other communal living situation. Keep in mind, however, that your child will still need one-on-one attention from you — possibly less of it, but not always.

In the nuclear family the child often finds himself with no one but Mom or Dad and maybe a sibling. There is nobody else to play with or to experience the sense of belonging with. Playing alone is not the answer, although it is fine to the degree that the child enjoys it. We need not be afraid of providing the kind of belonging and activities that are typical of a small modern family. One-on-one attention is the loving response to a child who has mostly only you to play with. Giving a child focused attention need not contradict the sense of community as long as there is balance and the child witnesses caring for each family member.

We must embrace the present and find the new qualities that it enhances in human beings. If we love what is, all other values fall in place gracefully no matter what the social structure is. The result of growing up in the nuclear family, with personal attention, is a different type of human being than the one being raised as part of a tribe; it brings forth different possibilities and qualities. Reading a book to a child or following his quests does not make a self-centered monster out of him; it provides for the development of individualized kind of thinking. The child grows up to belong to our society, a society which values individuality and the creative contribution of each person to the community at large. Neither system is better nor worse; these are just ways of being human, to celebrate and to cherish.

The fear of being child-centered is similar to other fears of "spoiling" children with love, cuddling, generosity, and kindness. You do not need to hold back your love for fear of spoiling your child. While being alone with Mom, if his need for relating is refused, a child only learns to be uncaring and to feel worthless.

Another premise of the tribe that many parents wish to imitate is letting a toddler hang around adult activities, which he then becomes skillful in and gradually joins. Here again, life has changed; the type of activities the child can observe at home, often executed by one stationary parent (at the computer, desk, sink, etc.), lack the interest and stimulation he needs. Some of the basic skills he wants to learn require personal interaction while others are not even in the same field as what he observes at home.

In the nuclear family the young child is conditioned to need one-on-one attention, which is neither bad nor good; it is just the current reality to enjoy and thrive on. With such an upbringing, children have the potential to grow up into independent thinkers and innovators like Einstein, Edison, and Mozart. They develop into compassionate adults because they experienced kindness, generosity, and love, and they become creative thinkers because their individual path is nurtured.

A child embraces with enthusiasm whatever culture he is born into. Nature made humans very pliable and capable of growing up well in more than one way. To pass on a love of life and inner peace we must embrace the way it is rather than wish for a different lifestyle; meet the child's needs as they occur in response to this society, and celebrate the qualities it does bring out. Happiness is the result of choosing what is. It would ease our anxieties if we embrace and cherish what we hand down to our children and let our love flow unhindered.

Distinguishing Your Needs From Your Child's

When you think you do everything that would nourish your child with love, yet she seems to doubt that you care about her, consider the possibility that you are directing her life even if you are not aware of doing so. When you direct your child's life or any part of it, she might feel like a vehicle for your needs.

Often we confuse our own needs with caring for the child, and we project these needs on the child.

Grandma Mary was visiting for the summer. Her two grandchildren (eight and four) were happily spending the days in unpredictable ways. Grandma became agitated. She suggested ways to organize the day for her grandchildren. She was concerned that they were "demoralized" due to lack of structure. She was talking about it incessantly and explaining to her son, Jack, that he must provide structure.

Initially Jack took it lightly, but when his mother wouldn't let go of the subject, he realized that he must do something. Using the S.A.L.V.E. formula (as explained in Chapter One), he took a minute to separate (S) his own reaction from what his mother's need may be by observing his inner conversation about it.

The thoughts he observed were: "She is wrong. I am right. The children are fine. She doesn't approve of me as a parent." He realized that these thoughts could not be proven and were not useful for his mother or for him. He also noticed that he himself was looking for his mother's approval about parenting. He smiled to himself and was then able to put his attention (A) on his mother. He thought about the fact that in her own home she was used to structured days, and he could see how unstructured vacation may be uncomfortable for her and the children's self-directed days hard to be with.

After listening (L) to his mother and validating (V) her perception, Jack thought of ways to make the days more structured without forcing the children to do anything they didn't want to. In the coming days he offered his mother opportunities to have some plans in her days (E). He invited her to help with cooking, and each day he came up with some outing or activity that broke the day conveniently and predictably. After a couple of days of having some structure in her days, Grandma said: "You see, I was right. In the last week the children had structure to their days and they look much happier."

Like Jack's mother, we all are sometimes convinced that we know what is best for the child, yet it is more likely to represent our own needs. Our emotions and mind-chatter are potent and can blind us from seeing the child's path; if we impose our view on her life, she doubts our love. You can easily recognize such situations, as when you find yourself upset with your child, driven by a strong will to make her do what you think is right. The word "should" is usually part of your complaint: "She should clean her room," "She should finish her food," "She should not interrupt," "She should cut her hair," etc. All these expectations represent what you need her to do in your "movie" about her. It has little to do with what is best for the child. To know about your child, listen to her.

Take time for self-examination (S of S.A.L.V.E.) and separate your need from your child's. Once you are clear whose need it is that drives you, be honest about it. You can say, "I have a need for your room to be clean;" you might ask for her help and, if she feels truly free to choose, she will probably say "no" until, sometimes, she may offer to help. If she does not choose to help meet your need, you can clean the room, leave it messy, or come to a mutual agreement that both you and your child are authentically excited about.

You can take it a step further and check your honesty with yourself. In this example, you may have a thought that children's rooms should be orderly, a concern that you are not a good parent if your child's room is a mess, or a vision that other homes are orderly. If you examine these ideas for relevance and truth, you may find yourself at peace with the child's mess or you may enjoy organizing it for your own sake.

Your child will feel connected by love when you are straight with her about your needs and you avoid controlling her or teaching her how to be. Cherish her choices and communicate yours. Indeed, loving your child is being ecstatic about who she is, celebrating her ways of being and her choices. This means that there are no expectations to stand in the way of the joyous celebration of the child. In the words of Leo Buscaglia: "Love never gives direction, for it knows that to lead a man off his path is to give him our path which will never be truly right for him. He must be free to go his own way."[2]

Confusing our need with a child's direction often occurs in the area of education. When wishing to support a child in her own self-generated quest, we feel invested in her success and unclear as to what is an act of love. "Do I let my child quit her team, or does love mean supporting her to go for her intended goal?" What is it that a child wishes to receive from her parents in those tough times? Indeed, nothing in parenting (and in life) is clear-cut. Instead, each child and each situation is unique.

Be consistent with loving your child and always ask yourself, "Is it her wish or mine?" And if it is yours, examine its validity honestly by checking with reality. For example, if your child hides the truth and you say that she lies, your underlying thought is that "she should not lie." That thought gets in your way of loving your child. If she lies, then she should lie, and you can then find out why she is afraid to tell you the truth.

Then you can rebuild the trust between you so she can feel safe to talk to you, no matter what.

If a child has a goal and needs your support in facing challenges along the way, loving her may mean standing for her commitment and not for her temporary fear or resignation. Deciding if this is the case may seem difficult, because each child is a sensitive individual and each relationship is a unique one. Yet, if trust between you is intact, you have a good chance of being able to sort things out with the child and to distinguish your desires from her authentic needs by listening and validating her fears. When her feelings are fully expressed and listened to, she is most likely to regain clarity about her aspiration and know how to proceed. Here are some examples:

> *Jack, sixteen-years-old and home schooled, told his parents that he was ready to leave home and have new experiences out in the world. He said he wasn't happy at home any more. After discussing his precise needs, his father, Kevin, plunged into a search for opportunities. He searched online and made many phone calls to find a safe and nurturing path for his son. He found an opportunity to travel in Europe and get college credit, a study bus tour for a semester, an alternative and wonderful boarding school, and other exciting opportunities.*
>
> *Kevin presented the material to his son and said, "Why don't you look over these sites and catalogues and get back to me when you have some clarity or questions about making your plans. We can look for other possibilities, too, of course." Jack took the pile of information with no enthusiasm. He did nothing with it.*
>
> *Two weeks went by. Jack seemed happy and on a new page.*

*"Any thoughts on your plans?" asked his
father finally.*

*"No, not really..." he said, then paused. "I'd like to
stay home for now. I feel excited about my life here and
my friends."*

By flowing with his son's expressed need, Jack's father
showed trust and support. This provided Jack with freedom
and clarity to choose. Such trust and responsiveness gives
access to choice with young children too.

*Four-year-old Iris was playing on the sandy beach
when she started throwing sand and crying, "I wanted
to stay with Grandma." Grandma lives in another state
and they had just come back from a long visit there.
Toward the end of their visit with Grandma, Iris
became homesick and they shortened their visit for
her sake.*

"I wanted to stay with Grandma," Iris cried.

*"Okay," Mom said, "I have my cell phone with
me. Would you like me to call and order airplane tick-
ets to go back right away?" She picked up her phone
and waited for Iris to decide. Iris looked thoughtful and
was silent for a long minute. Then she said, "No. Don't.
I want to stay here." She went back to the sand and in
no time was absorbed in her play.*

What if Iris had said yes? Although this is not likely, Mom
could have discussed with her the details so that together they
could sort things out and see if the trip would really be possible. Iris's mom didn't have to play the phone game; she could
have simply validated, "I hear that you want to go back to
Grandma's." Yet young children often respond well to freedom

of choice; presenting the opportunity to buy the plane ticket created instant clarity for Iris.

Sometimes the situation calls for a tougher kind of support. A child may freely choose a goal, yet, when obstacles or fear show up, she is ready to bag it. Should we support her fear by saying, "Sure, just quit your diving lessons," or do we support her original quest, and if so, how? In a counseling session a mother shared with me an experience that illuminates such a situation:

> *Brenda chose to take ballet and excelled in her class. A few years later she was the shining star of her ballet school. However, when the instructor suggested that she audition for the youth ballet company, Brenda said she didn't want to and that she hated the idea. She even talked about quitting dance altogether. Her practice time diminished and she seemed disinterested in dance.*
>
> *"I don't know if this is a call for freedom and trust, or whether Brenda is just scared of failing," her mother, Nancy, said. "Does she really want to quit, or is she counting on me to hold her vision for her in the face of her fear and self-doubt?"*
>
> *"Did you ask her about her feelings and thoughts?" I asked.*
>
> *"Yes. She admits that she is scared but she also says that she doesn't care about dance anymore and that being in the dance company will be horrible."*
>
> *"Have you showed your trust in her choice? And if you did, was she feeling at peace with not going for the audition and quitting dance?" I asked.*
>
> *"I told her that it is up to her. She didn't respond and didn't cancel the audition. She is being vague. I really think that she is eager to dance in the company but is scared."*

I suggested to Nancy to listen to Brenda's thoughts and feelings and acknowledge those, not as truth and drama, but as mind material. This can empower her to distinguish who she really is from her inner voice. "Only if Brenda becomes able to act in spite of fear will she have a real clue to her own aspiration," I explained. "If she makes her choice based on being scared, it is not a free choice, but one dictated by her fear. This kind of choice will be followed by regret and even depression if it does not represent her true intent."

"What if it does represent her true desire to let go of dance?" Nancy asked.

"Once she has fully expressed her feelings, she will be able to make her choice free of the dictate of fear. She knows what she wants. If she wants to dance she will choose it in spite of the fear; if not, she will quit and be at peace with her choice."

Nancy listened to Brenda's feelings. She did not offer advice or take action; she offered only validation and told her once that she thought there was a good chance that she would be accepted. She also reassured Brenda that her dance is her own agenda and that Nancy loves her no matter what she decides and regardless of the audition's outcome.

Brenda went to the audition of her own free will, all along saying that she didn't want to and that she hated it and that she hoped to fail the audition. If Nancy said, "So, are you canceling your audition?" Brenda would shrug and take no action.

Brenda was accepted to the dance company and got a medium-size role in the first production. She loved every minute of it and raved about her experience constantly while at the same time doing her best to look disinterested in the eyes of her parents.

Sometimes a human being, at any age, expresses disinterest in what she actually wants, or she wishes to save dignity by saying that she doesn't care if she won't pass an audition (just in case she is not accepted). You need not support her fear, only listen to it. Listening to her feelings and doubts will support her to stay in integrity with herself and to make her choice not from a place of fear, but from her power and vision of herself.

When A Child Doubts Your Love

Children form their feelings based mostly on the way they are treated and from a self-centered point of view. Therefore, when you say to your child upon his request to be with you, "Not right now, sweetie, I am busy," look at his face to check whether he does not sink into sadness. If you ask him if he's sad and he says, "It's all right," take the cue from his facial expression, not from his words. Do the corners of his lips bend down? Is he silent and serious? Is he pretending to be cool, or do you recognize other signs of hurt or of fear of losing your approval?

When your child is unsure of your love, the littlest rejection throws him into despair. He may think, "I knew it, she doesn't love me, I am just worthless." On the other hand, when a child feels secure in your love, he can handle an occasional delay of attending to his needs (when he is old enough), because it does not resonate with repeated past experiences. When we give too many experiences of "no love," the child can lose that emotional resilience. Once such phrases as "She doesn't love me" or "I am not good enough" become permanent in the child's brain, he tends to explain everything you do in a way that proves his assessment. In other words, he invents his life story based on your actions and words. It is his invention, but you are a player in his drama.

You cannot control your child's mind but you can learn to be aware of his "story making" style. When you have to deny your toddler your attention while nursing his little sister, see in his eyes what his conclusions may be. Is he concluding, "She doesn't love me…" or "I am not good enough…"? Many adults live with self-doubt they formed early on in response to their parents' unintended negation of their needs. Although much of these life experiences cannot and need not be prevented, when you are aware of what your child may be feeling, you can validate his experience and empower him to transform his conclusion: Instead of "She doesn't love me," he may then be able to say to himself something like "I hate waiting for the baby to nurse. But I know Mom loves playing with me. Once the baby is asleep Mom will be with me, so I am excited."

A baby will let you know if he feels fearful when you set him down to sleep in a cradle, far from the comforting sound of your breath and the feeling of your touch. He may also feel isolated and scared when not held as much as he needs. If fear or old cultural concepts stop you from embracing your baby in your arms and in your bed as much as he wants, he may doubt your love and his own worth.

A toddler may fear that you don't want him when you hug the baby. He can experience himself as rejected every time you tell him to stop what he's doing, when you speak on the phone and ignore him, when you use words that judge him, or when you expect something of him that he cannot fully accomplish.

An older child may doubt your love when your expectations of him do not match his own, when you have no time for him, when you protect a younger sibling from him, when you criticize him, or even when you praise him. It may sound strange that a child, commended for an achievement, would doubt his parent's love, but he might be thinking that you wouldn't be so "loving" if he had not somehow impressed and pleased you on your terms.

Many times a day we give children the message: You are not as important as something else (phone call, visitor, dinner, etc.), you are lower on my priority list. Our expressions of love are not always enough to make up for the insults of the day. And our deep love may be unknown to the child who has concluded otherwise, based on these experiences.

A child cannot experience himself as loved while he feels helpless, intimidated, or unable to express who he really is, and when he doubts his parents' appreciation of him. He may act like the person we expect him to be because he assumes that love means succeeding in pleasing us and getting approval. Yet a child cannot perceive being loved when he is not feeling safe to express himself fully and authentically. This is why control (whether by praise and rewards or by threats and punishment), and its resulting fear, get in the way of feeling connected by love.

A child who doubts his parents' love may sink into despair, which can manifest in insecurity and stress-based behaviors. In turn, these behaviors can provoke parental anger, which then hurts the child. Now he has the proof that he is not good and that his parents don't love him, which leads to more symptoms of despair.

To avoid slipping into this vicious cycle we must look past the child's behavior to the unexpressed pain that triggered it. The more destructive his behavior, the greater is his need for love and reassurance. Other manifestations of doubting parental love are: unhappiness, disinterest in doing things, problems in speech or learning, bed-wetting, tics, sleep disorders, aggression, eating disorders, general tension, and irritability. When a child feels completely secure in parental love, he has no need for such expressions; he feels self-confident and spends his time pursuing his passions.

Healing Your Ability to Love Unconditionally

If you had to please and impress your parents to earn their love, you may now feel reluctant to give love unconditionally. When your child's behavior evokes your anger or frustration, your past pain may block your ability to feel love and to notice his underlying need. It is possible to break this generational vicious cycle and let love flow. When you are unable to separate your own emotional reaction from your child's need, you may block your love and defend your right to scold, reject, or neglect him. In other words, scolding the child and thinking that he is the subject of your anger is your defense mechanism, which helps you avoid your own feelings. It is your mind in action; it is running the show from your past while you are, in a way, not conscious and not in charge.

Write down the thoughts that fuel your feelings and your intentions, and investigate them as you learned in Chapter One. To help you with your self-realization, notice the defenses that get in the way of loving are rooted in fears. The following are some of the more typical thoughts and beliefs that get in the way of love, and helpful ways of looking at them and freeing oneself from their grip.

Relieving the Fear of Losing Control

Many parents express fear of losing control, of being taken advantage of, or of raising children who have no sense of boundaries and consideration for others. When driven by these fears, parents use love like a reward. The child's compliance is then only a result of fear of not getting approval. This is one way fear passes from parent to child.

Letting go of these parental fears can be a matter of choice and of conscious work on oneself over years. It starts with recognizing what you are afraid of and letting the fear be present so you won't need to hide away from it by controlling another or by missing your child's need. Then you can shine a "brutal honesty" beam on the thought that produces your fear. Will he really never learn to help? Do you really believe that he will stay in diapers? Never learn manners? Won't learn to read... unless you coerce him to do it now? Once you realize that your thoughts are not reality, you can act without them and respond to the present expression of the child.

The fear of being taken advantage of is common among parents. The following example occurred in one of the family counseling workshops in our home.

Three-year-old Pete was eating scrambled eggs next to his mom. After a few bites he stopped and said, "Mommy, feed me."

Sandy hesitated. Pete had been eating by himself for a while now. She felt uncomfortable and said, "You can eat by yourself. You are three now."

"But, Mommy, I want you to feed me."

Sandy offered her hand and said, "Here, take my hand and you make me feed you." She tried to get him to participate in her solution, but he refused.

In our discussion later that day, Sandy was revealing her fear about being controlled and manipulated by her son.

"If you had no concerns about it, would you have fed your child?" I asked.

"Of course," she responded quickly and with a big smile. "I would enjoy feeding him. He would have giggled and we would have gazed at each other happily." Realizing that her own thinking, and not Pete, was the cause of her fear, Sandy reclaimed her power. This was in her hands, not his.

That evening Pete asked his mother to put his pajamas on and hold him to fall asleep in her arms. She did. As he fell asleep, tears started rolling down her cheeks. Later she put him in bed and said, "Usually he takes very long to fall asleep. This was so different, so peaceful and tender."

Sandy went on to explain how she used to hesitate in responding to Pete's needs to be cared for. "He is such a contrary child. I don't want him to stay so needy or to get used to me serving him all the time," she explained.

"What do you mean by contrary?" I asked.

"He goes against..." Sandy started, then stopped. "Oh, I see," she continued. "Do you mean that it is I who is contrary?"

"Well, who is it?"

"I negate his choices and I call him contrary."
Sandy laughed as she realized that what she saw in her child was really the teaching she needed to follow. She wanted to stop being contrary with her child.

After the session Sandy resolved to respond to Pete's requests for care and observe her fearful inner conversation about it without obeying it. Within two days she reported that Pete *"became"* a considerate and cheerful child and that they both enjoy a lot of cuddling and loving. She said, *"You know, this is strange, I was hesitating to respond to my child's plea for my love, yet I often feel just as afraid to draw the line and stop him from doing harm or from messing up my things. I can't assert myself when he takes aggressive actions and then I get upset and angry with him."*

"What is the fear?" I inquired.

"I don't know."

"What can happen?"

"He won't listen and I will feel defeated and helpless."

"Do you really believe he won't respond?"

"Not really," she said, *"I think I am afraid for myself."*

"Yes."

"That I don't deserve love."

Sandy paused and looked out the window. Her eyes filled with tears and she said, *"As a child I was convinced that my mother didn't love me because I wasn't good enough. I just felt I didn't deserve to be cared for. Now I am afraid to give love to my child and I don't dare to make requests for my own sake either."*

When you notice yourself holding back love or not daring to provide clear guidance, you can ask yourself, "What am I afraid would happen?" Let your inner voice express itself on paper and investigate the thoughts that separate you from your child. Put your thoughts of fear under the light of "truth." Over time and with repetition, your mind will learn to take these old reactions as material to be investigated, not as guidelines to act on in the present. You can then achieve ease in both loving your child fully and in loving and asserting yourself.

When you hold your love back due to your fears, the child may feel hurt and act desperately. You then may think his behavior is proof that your fears were right and you should not give even more. When that occurs, stop yourself and realize that his behavior is only proof that he is scared too. It is the fear of losing your approval that leads a child to aggression and desperate acts. Not being approved translates in his young mind to being unworthy and unloved. In contrast, it is the security in parental love that leads to peaceful and caring people. Just like air, we notice our need for love only when it is missing. When abundant, we take it for granted and we flourish. Realizing that the fear is a thought, not a reality, we are free to act without its guidance. This allows us to soak love in when given to us and pass it on with the same ease.

Relieving the Fear to Give Guidance

Many parents are able to bestow love on their children unconditionally. Some of these parents experience fear only in the area of providing clear guidance. Children experience love easily when they can rely on clear parental guidance.

> Ya-Fei was beside herself with despair when she called me. She said that she couldn't take her nine-year-old son to his activities because his younger brother,

*who was seven, refused to leave the house or to let her
go while he stayed with Dad.*

*"He is just fine once we go. He is actually happy.
But I can't do it anymore at all. I can't leave. If I try,
Leo is so mad that he breaks things, locks himself in
the bathroom, and throws a fit."*

*"What is the truth about your ability to go?"
I asked.*

"I can go, but I am afraid of Leo's fits."

*"And do you think he is benefiting when he can
prevent you from going?"*

*"Not really," Ya-Fei replied. "I don't know what
he wants."*

"What do you want Ya-Fei?"

*"The children's needs contradict each other. I don't
know what I want."*

*"Yes," I said, "which is the reason he is confused by
you and is trying so hard to bring clarity into his life."*

"So he is just reflecting my inability to lead the way?"

"Yes."

*Ya-Fei felt relieved and clear when the phone ses-
sion ended.*

"So, how did it go?" I asked in the following session.

*"I told Leo in advance that we wouldn't go much
so he could stay home a lot. I also told him that when
his brother has to be somewhere, we will be going and
he can join us or, when possible, he can stay with Dad
or the baby-sitter.*

*"He just came with us. There was no problem. I
couldn't believe it. He even took a toy with him on his
own and walked over to the car before I did."*

When we give clear guidance the child can count on, she
leans against the walls we provide and is free to explore and to
grow. She doesn't have to struggle to know what to expect.

A child can also handle diverse ways of growing up when she knows her family's culture, love is constant, she feels safe to express herself, and she knows what to expect. Indeed, within the context of love and respect, children have successfully been raised into thriving adults, despite many different cultural and economic conditions.

Moses and Adam are two young people I had the privilege of hosting in my home. Moses stayed with us for a few days as a part of a student exchange program and Adam as a homeschooling traveling guest who stayed with us for one summer. Both kept in contact with us over the years.

Moses was fifteen when he stayed with us. He grew up in a Native American family with a strict environment. He was self-confident, responsible, kind and expressive. He radiated inner beauty and emotional strength. He cherished the family that he grew up in and was passionately teaching us about his culture's ways and traditions. He spoke about finding out how different he was than his school peers; not only did he accept these differences between himself and his classmates, but held them with pride. He cherished what his parents gave him; the strict rules of behavior in his home were supported by constant love and were not erratically enforced.

Adam, on the other hand, came from a home of freedom and equality. I was deeply moved by his ability to connect and be vulnerable. His sense of humor broke any tension into laughter without anyone ever being put down. Like Moses, Adam found himself different from his peers. He believed that not being affected by peer pressure was his strength. He prided himself in being his own person. "It doesn't matter what others think of me. It only matters that I am at peace with myself," he explained.

These boys have the confidence that comes with clarity. Make the context of living together clear to your child so she need not waste her energy fearing outcomes or figuring out the guidelines; instead, she will be able to enjoy and utilize life fully. Fear of asserting ourselves as parents gets in the way of love.

Being clear about the way a family operates means that if a child has full and equal rights and full exposure to much of what the culture offers, then she needs clarity on how to be safe, how to get your advice, how to respect the freedom of others, and what she can count on when feeling at a loss. If, on the other hand, a child grows with individual freedoms some clear boundaries in terms of exposure or family lifestyle, then she must have guidelines on family decision-making, and on how her social world operates, who is in charge of what, and how to blaze her trail autonomously.

Whatever you create as your family culture, be straight about it and your child will strive to fit in confidently. Be straight also about your effort to distinguish your defenses from your authentic ability to love. A child has a lot of room for your fallibility as long as you are open and honest.

Relieving the Fear of Scarcity

One of the greatest fears we live with is the fear of not having enough love or other things and conditions that represent love. This is the result of receiving bits and pieces of love conditionally when we were children and because the whole culture is permeated with the idea that receiving goodness is conditional. A child in this society is likely to see a lot of exchange of goods and services and not so much giving for its own sake. The result is tension in relating to one another: "Will my kindness pay back? What's in it for me?" Yet, kindness always pays back because giving is the payback.

If you didn't receive enough attention, affection, or other expressions of love as a child, you may have experienced love as something to struggle for. To use the air analogy: If love was conditional, then most likely you were constantly "gasping" for love. This experience may block your ability to let go of your defenses and of your fear that you won't get what you need. It hinders the ability to receive and to give. This inner voice of fear can be so loud in your mind that you may find it hard to be in the moment with your child. Yet, bringing yourself to the here and now with your child is the best way to free yourself from the tyranny of these old records about scarcity. Observe what your mind is saying, investigate its validity, and explore how you would be without the particular belief. Then see whether the lesson your mind has for your child could benefit you in some way. When you gain clarity, put your attention on your child (S and A of S.A.L.V.E.).

You can't get any closer to God or to that which we cannot understand than through loving. Creation puts in your hands the responsibility of nurturing a human being into maturity. You must do so without turning the child into your creation, which will only choke the magic of her being. Treat your child with reverence and you need no parenting manuals.

Love flows abundantly and limitlessly, as long as we don't get in the way. Controlling the flow of love is like closing the gate and deciding how much the next in line is going to get. Letting love flow means keeping both ends open. When your commitment to the child is greater than your personal fears, you will grow beyond your limitations and your child will flourish.

Nurturing Self-Love (The Fear of Asserting Oneself)

To free the flow of love toward your child, you need to love and appreciate yourself. By loving yourself, you make it easy for people to love you, further increasing the stream of love in its flow toward your child. Giving can only be accomplished when someone is receiving. Therefore, receiving is an act of love.

The perception of scarcity and conditional love as children has left many parents unable to keep the gates of love swinging both ways. They may feel needy and find it hard to give love, or, they may reject love to various degrees, perceiving themselves as undeserving or embarrassed. Not receiving unconditional love as children, many adults spend much money and time chasing love substitutes in food, goods, TV, glory, and other self-soothing strategies. When feeling insecure about their own worth, parents tend to be unassertive and therefore hesitate to give clear guidelines to a child.

You owe it to your child to heal yourself and to close the door on the past. Use the investigation process offered in this book to explore and enlighten yourself about the way your own mind deceives you, so you can reclaim yourself. Use counseling, group work, transformational events, books, art, or any other avenue that suits you to build your self-esteem, and to bring forth your ability to be present and flow with what is in front of you. (See the "Resources" section at the end of the book for more information on self-realization work.) Rekindling unconditional self-love will free you to give love and, further, you will feel nurtured by giving.

Becoming a parent requires taking a quantum leap from feeling nourished by self-gratification to feeling nourished also by the gratification of another. It is the path of learning to move away from resistance, to embracing what the moment presents you with. The more you are sure of your worth, the less you need to focus on yourself and to negate your child's choices. Feeling secure in your own value and being unconcerned with gaining love makes you free to love your child and to be able to enjoy your contribution to her life. In addition, being liberated from the need to gain worth by impressing others or depending on their appreciation ensures that in tough moments, in public or with Grandma, your love toward your child dictates your actions and not your concern about impressing anyone.

Although living with children demands us to mature and get beyond the point of devoting our lives to our own desires, we do need to give attention to our own satisfaction. As you nourish and support the development of another human being for the fulfillment of her dreams, your own aspirations get nurtured in direct and indirect ways; but her dreams are not yours, nor are they the fulfillment of your agenda. As you join your child's journey, your own growth is enhanced in unpredictable ways that you will eventually put into your own path. A mother told me how mothering has created her personal career.

The mother of a baby and a toddler, Dorothy, called me when she was feeling sad about her own career, which she said was fading away. She had stopped playing the violin, dancing, and acting. She was committed to providing for her children's needs fully, including co-sleeping, tandem nursing, and avoiding daycare and baby-sitters. She was also planning to homeschool them. At the time she called me she was able to go to a dance class once a week, but nothing else.

We often hide behind old needs as a way to avoid moving into the present. I encouraged Dorothy to explore the truth about what it was she wanted for herself at that time.

"I want to enjoy my children," she said, "but I also miss the me that used to be."

"Would you enjoy your children better without missing the way you were?" I asked.

"Yes, that would be such a relief," Dorothy said promptly. "Thinking that I am missing something hurts. But how do I know I am not missing anything?"

I suggested to Dorothy to flow with life and explore her real passions in the present rather than be attached to wanting what she had in the past.

The following week Dorothy reported that she was singing while doing other things and with the baby in the sling.

A few years later Dorothy was taking voice lessons and singing in a choir. She said she had never enjoyed music more. Then her second child became interested in musicals and Mom and daughter ended up together on stage, singing, dancing, and acting.

When I acknowledged her achievement, Dorothy remarked, "The best part is that I have matured in ways that nothing but parenting could have given me. Not only do I enjoy my stage in life, but I have an ability to trust the way life evolves and to cherish each *moment; this enriches my marriage and all my relationships and experiences."*

And another similar story:

A father who let go of his established job to raise his son told me how, when money ran out, he decided to start his own business from home because he loved being part of his son's life. His computer programming business was thriving when he last talked to me, and he said that not only was his work much more interesting than what he used to do, but his son was already an expert programmer at age thirteen.

When we feel sad about what we leave behind, it is only because we are dwelling on our past. In the present there is always change, which is satisfying when you are aware and engaged in it here and now. New possibilities emerge all the time, but when the mind clings to the way it used to be, you are not likely to notice and enjoy what comes your way. Going toward the unknown is the nature of being alive. The fear of letting go of the past gets in the way of fully enjoying our children in the present. Once you have children, life will never be the same again; it will be different, rich, and constantly changing. As long as you flow with it creatively and celebrate change, you will enjoy one of the best rides available to human beings.

While you have to take care of yourself, you need not focus on you. Taking care of at least some of your needs can be done side by side with your child, while focusing your attention on him. At the same time, your ability to enjoy giving love and attention to your child is directly linked to caring for yourself. You are doing it for you, for your own enjoyment. To rejuvenate your joy of parenting, you can take some time by yourself or with a friend; even ten minutes a day can help you enjoy rather than resent your child's constant needs. But mostly, notice what you say to yourself that causes the impatience or resentment. Find out which of your thoughts causes you pain and which ones enhance your ability to love and to live with your child.

Contentment comes from being present; when you read your child a book while wishing to tend to the garden, you deprive both of you of much joy. It is your own thought that takes you away from the joy of the moment. Either, take your child to the garden to care for it first, or read the book and save the thought about the garden till later. Cherish the moment; let yourself be washed by the love and awe you feel toward your child. If your mind is in the garden, you will miss it.

Parents often tell me how one day they suffer while caring for their child, yet the next day, doing the same thing, they enjoy themselves immensely. The difference is in choosing to be where you are. In other words, you can be with your child and be upset (wanting to be elsewhere), or you can be with your child and be happy. What will help you to stay present is detecting the thoughts that take you away, writing them down, and exploring their effect on you.

Naturally, most parents do not arrive at parenting already skilled at what it takes. We seem to evolve "on the job," and this fact is yet another aspect we learn to cherish. Don't miss the "ride" by attempting to mold your child to your limitations; instead, living with children gives you the opportunity to keep breaking through those limitations so you can become more loving.

In a phone session, Robin made that kind of choice for herself:

> *Eight-year-old Ayla had the habit of repeating words and phrases incessantly while jumping and talking endlessly. Robin, her mother, couldn't stand it and kept stopping her daughter's happy chatter.*
>
> *I asked Robin what she feels when the urge to stop her daughter's repetitive talk overcomes her.*
>
> *"I feel irritated and impatient. I want quiet. I want to be left alone."*
>
> *Robin was convinced that her need was the truth, the right thing, and that her child should learn to stop herself for Mom's sake. She wanted me to teach her better ways to control her daughter.*
>
> *"Ayla's behavior stimulates your discomfort. Are you sure you want to limit her?" I asked, "Or, would you like to free yourself from this sense of annoyance and have some freedom to listen and to be delighted with your daughter?" I asked.*
>
> *"Of course I want the freedom. Right now I have no control over my urge to stop her. No choice. I am forced by my inner voice to stop her. It doesn't work. She resents me and I feel guilty and disconnected," Robin said.*
>
> *"When you surrender to your inner voice and you stop your child, what do you get to avoid?" I asked. "If she kept talking, what would you feel?"*
>
> *Robin's voice was trembling. "I don't know what it is. I just know that I am crying."*
>
> *"Yes," I said, "I understand. Tune into the sadness."*
>
> *"My mom always wanted me to stay away. She wanted to rid herself of me," Robin recalled. "I felt like a nuisance to her. Now I am just like her. I feel the same about Ayla. I don't want to be a mom. But I do want to. I love her."*

"You want to want to be a mom?"

"Yes, that's it. But when I am, I want to run away."

"Are you scared of feeling your childhood loneliness again?"

Robin responded, *"Yes, the pain of being rejected by my mom. I never thought that I was shutting my child down in order to avoid my own old hurt. Now I have to choose between growing up or limiting my child."* She laughed, *"In essence, I force her to meet my needs and to cater to my limitations. Yes, I would love to become happy with Ayla's chatter and be done with that old pain."*

"Later you can explore your pain-producing thought that your mom rejected you," I suggested. *"You don't really reject your daughter, and your mother was most likely in a similar position. For now, however, let's stay with your painful thoughts about Ayla.*

"When the voice inside you says 'I can't stand it, she must stop,' take a minute to notice it; write it down and look at it. Do you really want to stop your child's bubbling and chatter?"

"No. I want her to be free."

"Can you imagine how you would feel when she bubbles like this if the thought that you are annoyed didn't cross your mind?"

"I don't know. I have never seen her being like this without having this thought."

"Imagine you have succeeded. Your daughter is accommodating and has stopped the repetitive chatter. How would you feel?"

"Oh my goodness, horrible! Oh, I see...so without the thought that it's annoying, I want her to keep being herself, free, alive, happy, expressive."

"When you are free from your thoughts, she is free too."

*"Yes. That's it. Without those thoughts, I just
love her."*
*"So can you see your expectation that she shouldn't
repeatedly chatter as your own lesson?"*
*"Oh yes. I will be happier if I stop my own repeti-
tive mind chatter. Wow! Yes! She is just being herself
and I can love her."*

Any time your limitations stand in the way of love and generosity, you have an opportunity to set yourself free. Can you love yourself enough to push yourself out of your own emotional prison? Just as you support your child to act in spite of her fears, so you can do for yourself. When you choose love over your old painful story, your child will learn to do the same for herself.

Expanding your own tolerance does not mean sacrificing and always bending your needs for the child. It means that you learn to distinguish between needs and limiting, old mind chatter. If you find yourself needing to control or to escape, observe these thoughts with love, but don't let those dictate your actions. Use a counselor or a friend to help you explore the validity of your thoughts to your child and to yourself. When a child sees you succumbing to emotional limitations she does not learn about self-love, but about weakness and fear. As she caters to your emotional limitations, she learns to fear emotions in herself and in others. A child can be considerate of your needs and be kind and generous to you when she experiences kindness and when she observes you taking care of yourself powerfully.

Feeling connected by love is not dependent on someone else giving "it" to you, either. The existence of a nurturing adult relationship in your life is a blessing but not a requirement. It is mostly your relationship to yourself that counts. Feeling emotionally satisfied is a function of being in the now and of appreciating yourself, which then enables you to cherish your child exactly the way she is and derive the greatest joy from watching her grow.

Loving yourself will also help you to keep your child free from the burden of providing love for you. Your child is not here to give you love and gratitude or to fulfill your dreams and aspirations. Her existence is naturally going to enrich your life and add meaning, love, and direction to it — but you cannot build your way of relating to your child on such expectations. The moment you find yourself having an agenda you wish your child would fulfill, you are meeting your own need, not your child's.

Some parents mix giving attention to the child with using her life to fulfill their own dreams. Focusing on the needs of another means providing for her so she can go her own way; it does not mean using her path for your aspirations. When you care for your child, focus on her and not on yourself; take care of yourself independently of providing for the child.

Joining your child's ride can be so incredibly joyful precisely because it is not about you. If you surrender to the "ride" you can be in the moment, free of your mind's noise. The freedom from your personal agendas allows for this amazing journey to unfold, as does a trip to a place you have never been to before. In fact, accompanying your child along her path is indeed a journey to a new land, which is nature's way of bringing you back to the moment.

Pleasing Our Parents

If, like most people, you have been conditioned to earn acceptance, you may find yourself choosing some of your parenting ways based on the need to live up to your parents' or others' expectations. In this domain too, building your own self-esteem either by yourself or with professional assistance can help you care for your child rather than for your image or for your parents. Loving your child means not compromising her needs for the impressions you make as a parent. In one of my workshops, a mother shared about her experience with this issue:

> At four years of age, Nathan was still in diapers. His parents trusted him and didn't want to make an issue of the subject.
>
> When Aunt Lily came to visit, she expressed her dismay and started talking to Nathan about using the toilet. One morning she said to him, "I will take you for a walk in the park if you use the toilet and then wear your clothes without a diaper." Nathan moved away and refused to go with his aunt.
>
> "Come on, you can do it. We will have fun and I will buy you a candy on the way," Aunt Lily said as she walked over to him.
>
> Although in disagreement with Lily's manipulative plot, Nathan's mother, Martha, joined and said, "It's all right, Nathan, you can try it. Maybe it is a good time for you to go without diapers and you will have fun."
>
> Nathan stood frozen. With his own mom not on his side he felt confused and helpless.
>
> "So?" said Aunt Lily.

> *Nathan looked again at his mom (hoping for sup-*
> *port). Then he ran away to his room crying.*

Martha's insecurity led her to go against her child's need. Even the most secure among us fall into the trap of pleasing our extended family and even strangers. It is not something to feel guilty about, but rather to notice, so we can diminish the times when our priorities are sacrificed. Martha did catch herself and shifted her direction.

> *Nathan came running out of his room and started*
> *pounding on his mother.*
> *"Oh, we don't hit," said Aunt Lily, but Martha*
> *signaled her to hold it and asked Nathan, "Are you*
> *upset because you need to make your own decisions*
> *about yourself?"*
> *"Yes, yes," he said. He stopped pounding and threw*
> *himself on the floor.*
> *"Would you have liked to make your own choices?"*
> *Martha asked and touched him gently.*
> *Nathan stopped kicking and said, "Yes, you don't*
> *love me. I hate you, Mom!"*
> *"When Aunt Lily invited you to go with her if you*
> *didn't wear a diaper, you wished that I would have*
> *told her not to bug you about it, is that it?"*
> *"Yes, you are MY mother, not hers," sobbed Nathan.*
> *"You are right. And, you can stay in diapers as*
> *long as you wish. I will tell Lily that you decide about*
> *your body."*
> *She turned to Lily. "Nathan needs to make his*
> *own decisions."*
> *"Well, okay," said Lily, "let's go on a walk and get*
> *a candy anyway."*
> *"I don't want to go," declared Nathan.*
> *The three of them made new plans for the afternoon.*

Loving a child is being on his side regardless of any impression we make on others. As a parent you are here to stand for your child's dignity and well-being. By honoring your child you will demonstrate to people present a new possibility that may inspire them.

Being Consistent

Parents often think that they must be consistent with their responses to their children. In attempting to be consistent they sometimes do things that hurt a child or create anger and disappointment because they fear that inconsistency will confuse her. Yet, the only consistency that matters is love. When your action is inconsistent with loving, the child is not only confused but also hurt and misguided. At that moment you are not true to your own loving self.

Change the rules, not the love; love needs to be the only consistent guide to our actions. Ask yourself: "Is my child experiencing me as loving her? Am I in touch with my love for her when I scold her, when I insist she clean her room, finish her homework, eat her food?" If your child obeys you and cleans her room while feeling resentful and worthless, is her clean room worth it? If she does her homework or her homeschooling studies, gets good grades, yet doesn't feel secure in your love, do her academic successes have value? Is anything more important than loving another human being so that they know it without a doubt?

"The Window"

by *Bruce Linton*

I was getting ready to go to work
to give a lecture
I was putting my notes in my briefcase
when the ball came through
the window
and the glass went flying,
a million tiny knives
all over the living room.
In that moment
I felt my anger grow inside,
my frustration at the house
never being organized enough,
the expense of getting
the window repaired,
living for a while
with cardboard or plywood
to replace the glass,
the thought of
how will we ever
clean up all the glass,
I became angrier still
as I now knew
I would be late for my presentation.

I heard your small four-year-old
feet running up the steps.
I saw your tiny arm
push open the door,
your eyes looked up to mine
moist, searching.
In that moment history changed.
I took you in my arms,
"Are you hurt,

it's only a window,
it can be replaced.
that you are not hurt,
is what is important to me.
It's only glass,
you are my son.
I love you.
Let's get the broom."[3]

I am often asked: Are children so sensitive that we have to "walk on eggshells" to preserve their emotional well-being? My answer is: No, we only need to "walk on" love. Children are able to endure rough times and mighty challenges as long as they take our love for granted and can express themselves fully. When they can walk on the carpet of love you spread under their feet, they will be resilient and resourceful.

Notes: Chapter Two

1. *Beloved Prophet: The Love Letters of Kahlil Gibran and Mary Haskell, and Her Private Journal* (Knopf, 1972)
2. Leo Buscaglia, *Love: What Life is All About* (Ballantine Books, Reissue 1996)
3. Bruce Linton, Ph.D. "The Window," a poem from *"Wife, Son, Daughter: A Father's Poems"* (Fathers Forum Press, Berkeley, CA, 1995; ISBN0964944138; with permission)

Chapter Three

༈

Self-Expression

Your child's emotional outbursts

The capacities to shed tears, to laugh, and to express feelings and thoughts with words are uniquely human. By expressing what is on our mind, we maintain our emotional well-being and gain freedom to move forward. Although some people are able to quiet their mind and move on, most of us live as though we are our mind and therefore need tools to deal with its reactions and hurts. Expressing ourselves is also our way of creating a connection with the people we love. Children express themselves not only to maintain their own emotional well-being, but also for their intellectual and social development.

Stopping a child from fully expressing his feelings does not stop the feelings, it only stops their expression. When a child feels unable or unsafe to express himself fully, his feelings accumulate until he is in a state of distress. This invariably leads to physical, behavioral, and developmental manifestations including aggression, depression, tics, compulsions, learning difficulties, sleep disorders, and more.

Most of us enjoy and even encourage our children's laughter, creativity, and other pleasing ways of self-expression. However, when a child gives vent to pain, anger, jealousy, loneliness, disappointment, or grief, we are apt to stop the healthy flow of feelings, thereby hindering his development and interfering with his emotional well-being. The tendency to look for ways to fix the situation can distract us away from noticing the child's need to unleash his feelings. Many small events, like a scraped knee, a canceled visit, an insult, or a disappointment don't require solutions even if the child reacts with tears or rage. Although we must avoid dramatizing and adding more to the child's response, we can calmly listen, validate, and let him be. He can then experience himself as capable of handling emotions.

When a child has been completely heard, his capacity to recover from ordinary emotional hurts is remarkably quick. He may need to express very little, or he may have a full-fledged tantrum. Either way, when he has the freedom to let his feelings be known in the ears of attentive and loving parents/adults, he can spring out of rage and tears into the next play as though nothing happened. The mind does not have, yet, as great a grip over the child as it does for most adults; he moves on easily, as long as we don't anchor his emotions by stopping their expression or by adding our reactions.

In the rare case that a child does persist in expressing his upset in spite of your supportive listening, you can assume that the present event has evoked other old, painful memories that were not fully cared for when they occurred. He is feeling safe in your presence and using your attention to clear old pain out of his system. He will then cry or rage longer and your attentive listening will allow the healing to occur. Later in this chapter you will find examples of the way a child uses an event in the present to unleash past hurts.

Avoid planting feelings in your child's mind. Wait for him to assess his own response to what happens. Such pronouncements as "Oh no, that hurts" before the child forms his own response or "You must be feeling sad" before a child assesses his emotions about the situation do not help him. He may grab what you offer, sometimes forming an attitude for the rest of his life. Trust your child. If he needs to express feelings, he will; if he doesn't, he won't. It is not for you to decide or to cause his expression or the lack of it. Whatever he does express will be authentically his. Don't teach him to feel upset if he is able to let go and move on, and if he shares himself or cries, validate his feelings without dramatizing. Most often children express themselves briefly and they are done; it is only our attempt to either stop them or dramatize their story that lengthens the process.

As a counselor I often hear stories of children's fast recovery. One example, related in Chapter One, illustrated the fast recovery of Orna from her upset about having to leave the pool. She felt ready to embrace the present as soon as her mother heard and validated her experience. When parents project their own worries, the child mirrors those feelings back to them by clinging to drama. Once parents learn to let the tantrum or sadness flow out freely, they observe with amazement how the child moves on.

Tamara called me to ask how to respond to her daughter Sarah's recurring rage. "The tower falls, she cries; the banana breaks, she shrieks. Everything is so upsetting to her."

I asked Tamara how she responds in these events.

"I try to fix things quickly. I replace the banana, rebuild the tower, or find a way to compensate her," she said.

"Is everything really so upsetting for your daughter?" I asked.

"It seems this way," Tamara said.

"Yes. You see her as unable to go through these situations because you believe your idea that she cannot handle it. But can you be sure that she cannot handle it and that she wants you to fix things?"

"No."

"So when you rush to her aid, thinking that she can't handle it, what are you feeling?"

"Oh I see," she said, bursting out laughing. "I feel unable to handle her frustration. I am the one for whom everything is so upsetting. Everything that happens to her is too upsetting for me. I panic. I fix everything for my own sake."

Once Tamara realized that her reaction was about herself and not about her child, she was able to see that her daughter was not the one needing help. She could see that Sarah needs to experience the fallen tower if she is to find out her own strength in the face of it; that she can cry over a canceled visit or an irreplaceable broken banana, and if Mom doesn't imply that it's too much for her, she will pass through it powerfully and know herself as able to feel, express, and move on.

Stopping her upset is actually the reason why Sarah may be feeling helpless and why she explodes over every little mishap; she will use any reason, no matter how small, to experience her own feelings fully. When being rescued she feels helpless; her agenda is thwarted. Experiencing herself as able to go through challenges will make her feel powerful.

The following week Tamara had a breakthrough; she told me that Sarah was painting a picture when the jar of water spilled and destroyed it. Sarah screamed and Tamara picked up the jar of water and was ready to offer compensation to stop the upset. Then she remembered to give attention to Sarah, and instead of pulling her out of her (safe) predicament, Tamara listened and validated.

"This was my best picture ever," Sarah yelled and threw herself on the sofa kicking and screaming.

"You want your picture dry," Tamara said and sat next to Sarah.

"Yes, I want it the way it was. I almost finished it."

"Are you worried that you won't be able to make another picture as nice?" Tamara asked.

"I can't make another one like this." Sarah turned her screams into sobs and Tamara offered to hold her. She refused but kept sobbing and gradually got closer to her mother.

She cried for a couple of minutes and then was quiet. Tamara said nothing but stayed attentive.

"I could see that Sarah was thinking and she seemed calm," Tamara told me. After a minute of contemplation Sarah got up and went to play with her doll. Later that day she even painted again and was excited about her creation.

Tamara made a huge shift from trying to alter reality for Sarah to supporting Sarah's ability to face reality. She joined and validated Sarah's experience rather than pulling her out of it; instead of denying her daughter's feelings with, "Oh never mind, you can make another picture," she listened and validated Sarah's likely concern. Valid feelings do not imply real facts. Sarah will be empowered to create other pictures, not by avoiding the feeling, but by making peace with her loss. Given the freedom to express her feelings, she moves on at ease. Happiness is what we experience when we cherish reality, not when we oppose it or expect to be rescued. A child learns to be content by experiencing the power of choosing what is.

The child who experiences our peaceful presence is bound to conclude that going through intense emotions is a part of being human. Being comfortable with his own emotions, he develops a sense of inner peace, knowing that he need not fear challenges and the feelings that may come with them. He learns to allow these experiences to go through him fully and resolve situations powerfully and responsibly. It is after the storm passes through that he can act with clarity and effectiveness.

Looking back, a child may even be able to recognize his own self as much more powerful than the negative "stories" his mind tells him, as twelve-year-old Luke did.

> *Luke was in our home for a family retreat. The previous evening he and I had a talk about the mind and how thoughts come in and we obey them and do things we don't want to do.*
>
> *Luke and his younger brother Timmy were at the kitchen table. All at once they both rushed to the piano and started shouting at each other while pushing each other off the piano bench.*
>
> *"I said I am going to play now; when I said it you ran to the piano and got there first. It's my turn," said Timmy.*
>
> *"I was going to play before you said it," responded Luke.*

"No, you ran just as I said it. You were in the middle of eating."

"I had the idea first, so I came first to the piano while you were talking."

All of a sudden Luke got up and left the piano. On his way to the other room he saw me. He smiled and said, "I caught myself. That was that silly mind story about bugging Timmy. I didn't really want to play the piano."

It is rare for a youth this young to be able to distinguish his righteous thoughts from his authentic self. You can empower such self-awareness by modeling and by flowing with, not against, his choice of expression.

The Courage to Feel

When giving attention to a sobbing or raging child, you may feel discomfort and even panic. You may perceive the child as suffering beyond her ability to cope. This perception, however, is really about your own discomfort. Therefore the rush to distract a child from her hurt or frustration, to compensate for a disappointment, or to minimize the importance of her plight is a response to your own anxiety, not the child's. It is not going to help her become emotionally resilient and capable of facing and resolving difficulties. She must experience living with emotional storms if she is to master them.

When you feel the impulse to stop the child's expression of unpleasant emotions, ask yourself what your purpose is. You may want to have her be happy all the time, because her pain is too uncomfortable for you and, you assume, for her. If "a scene" happens in public, you may worry about "looking good" as a parent. You may also have a need to stop her because you are in a hurry or you need clarity while feeling baffled by her outburst. Yet, when you prevent your child from expressing her hurt, she buries the pain while feeling bewildered and lonely. Meanwhile, you miss the opportunity to connect with her deeply and to know the causes of her distress. What she learns is to run away from feelings and to hide them from others; she internalizes a sense that she is too weak to experience any discomfort. In essence, with the best of intentions, many of us teach our children that hurtful feelings are scary and should be avoided.

Some men tell me that they don't have any issue with emotional expression and can let their child rage as she wishes. However, this is not what I am suggesting here. Being indifferent and ignoring the child's plea is not the same as giving loving attention. If you can stay "cool" in the face of your child's passionate expressions, you are more likely to be emotionally repressed than present with your child. The result for your child is the same as stopping her, because your indifference tells her that her feelings should not be expressed.

To grasp more fully how ineffective it is to distract children from their emotional turmoil, imagine that you have just learned that your mother is dying or your partner is filing for divorce. In desperation you visit a friend, yearning to talk, cry, or rage in a supportive environment. No sooner do you begin letting out your emotions than your friend offers advice or suggests a distraction: "Let's go to a movie, that will take your mind off it." You are more likely to wish that your friend would listen to you attentively, ignore telephone calls and other intrusions, and focus on you.

A child is a person with the same needs. If, as a child you were "rescued" from emotional turmoil by compensations and distractions, or if it was unsafe for you to express yourself, you may find it unsettling to be with your upset child. Yet, by listening to your sad or angry child while noticing your thoughts and emotions, you can recover your own ability to experience the full range of emotions rather than run away from them. You will then be able to explore the thoughts that fuel the specific emotions and start to understand how your mind works. By understanding the cause (thoughts) and effect (feelings and reactions), you will gain insight into yourself and grow in clarity. You will recover your ability to feel fearlessly, knowing that your anxieties are the grist for the mill of your own self-realization.

People fear painful feelings precisely because they were denied their expression. The denial of their emotions made those seem even more scary and potent, and as a result, most adults take feelings too seriously. In contrast, when safe to express themselves, children are able to accept emotions as part of being human. If we don't teach them that having a hurt feeling is a problem, they assume, correctly, that these experiences are part of life, that emotions are nothing to fear, dread, or avoid, nor make a grand fuss about. When expressed, feelings come and go. One can then make coherent choices that are not based in fear and avoidance of pain.

The following are some strategies parents use to stop a child's self-expression and ways to prevent them:

Denial

Denial is the primary method for shutting down a child's (or one's own) self-expression—a way most of us use habitually, simply because it was done to us. Denial is sometimes done by silence and avoidance, and in other times by words and distractions. When Lena was three years old, for instance, she was afraid of longhaired and bearded men, a feeling her mother initially dismissed.

> *One day when Lena was sitting in the back seat of the car, her father stopped to talk to an acquaintance with long, dark hair and a big mustache, whose face filled up the frame of the car window. Lena was quiet for a while and then anxiously asked, "Can we go now?" Without thinking, her mother said that the longhaired man was "a nice guy."*
>
> *"No, he's not!" Lena replied confidently. Clearly, she needed to express her discomfort and was not about to let her mother deny it.*
>
> *"Oh, I see," said her mother, realizing her error. "You don't like him."*
>
> *"No," said Lena, "I want to go."*
>
> *After they left the man behind, Lena said, "He is not really scary. I just don't like him."*

Lena was able to inquire into her own feelings because they were not denied or taken away from her. Her self-realization has likely helped her in recovering from this anxiety about bearded men.

Becoming familiar with your own habitual phrases of denial will help you catch yourself before you say them. Here are some examples of language that indicates denial of the child's feelings and expressions:

- "It wasn't that bad."
- "What's so upsetting about that?"
- "I don't see anything wrong with it."
- "It's not the end of the world."
- "Oh, it's nothing. You're all right."
- "Nothing happened."
- "It's okay. You're fine."

Children tend to feel perplexed, if not insulted, by such comments, because the words contradict their inner experience. To a child who feels scared or hurt, something did happen, everything is not okay, and the experience is upsetting. Instead of denial, you can use validation, which affirms the child's experience, or provide useful information when applicable. When a child cries after a fall, we can hold her and say, "Does the scratch hurt?" or "Are you afraid it will stay like this?" If she nods through her tears, we can reassure her with, "I know how painful it is right now; it will stop hurting soon." Mending her scraped knee is needed; stopping her tears or screams is not. Our task is to give her relevant information and to listen to her emotional expression (L of S.A.L.V.E.). We can let her know that she may cry as long as she needs to and that her emotion is valid. The empowerment (E of S.A.L.V.E.) comes from our benign attitude—from listening to her without engaging in her drama. The drama is the story a child may tell herself, like "I'll never be able to walk again." We don't want to give power to the mind's story. When we listen and validate her fear in a simple tone of voice and give useful information, she experiences our trust in her ability to move through the experience.

Denial is sometimes cloaked in lighthearted comments that rob the child of her autonomous right to feel and to trust her inner voice. When a child says, "Yuck, I don't want it," and we reply, "Oh, but it's yummy," we invalidate a decision she has made. If a six-year-old's quick glance at dinner elicits a desire not to eat or if she asks for a banana instead, she has made a choice that we are called upon to respect. If a teenager says that the coat you bought him is not "cool," his reality cannot be denied by conviction. When your toddler is at the playground, poised on top of a slide and frozen in terror, your words, "Don't be afraid. You can do it," contradict her emotional experience as she contemplates that long journey down. Indeed, self-trust and self-reliance are developing right there on top of the slide as she assesses the situation and arrives at a decision on her own. To empower her, just watch and be relaxed and confident. If she talks to you, show her that you know how she feels: "I hear that you are scared and not sure if you want to slide down. We are not in a rush. Take your time. It is up to you." Then just follow her lead whether to give a hand, to look away, or to carry her down.

Following are some typical phrases that deny the child's choice. Here again, becoming aware of your own phrases is the first step toward eliminating them:

- "Try it anyway."
- "Why don't you do it just this time?"

- "Try this one—it's better."
- "You don't want this piece of junk, do you?"
- "You had plenty of time to play." (When she wants to keep playing.)
- "You're tired." (When she wants to keep running.)
- "You must be hungry by now." (When she refuses to eat.)
- "But you love to play with Susan." (When she pushes her friend away.)
- "You can do it." (When in self-doubt.)
- "Don't be scared/shy/upset."
- "You don't need to cry."
- "But you will be cold." (When she takes off her coat.)

Even when a child has made a potentially dangerous choice, it is important to acknowledge the precipitating emotions. For instance, when your child runs after the cat into the busy street and you grab her with a scream, you can ask, "Were you worried that Jumbo was running away?" It is equally important to acknowledge the emotions aroused by your swift intervention: "Were you startled when I screamed and grabbed you so fast?" And after her response, you can hug her and share your own experience: "I was scared seeing you running into the street. I feel relieved holding you safely in my arms."

Parents tend to scold a child who took a dangerous step. By expressing anger, they hope to ensure that the child won't repeat the unsafe action. However, fear of parental anger is the wrong reason to avoid danger, and, dangerously, it is a reason that won't last. You want your child to care for her own safety based on understanding and on her desire to be safe. She will be moved by your feelings, and inspired by your trust in her. In a family counseling session, I learned about Connie's reaction to her daughter's unsafe action and how she connected with her by expressing herself vulnerably.

> *Two-year-old Jill was excited to watch the fire at her uncle's house. She had never seen a fireplace and her father explained why she must stay away from it. She watched her uncle from a safe distance as he was piling the wood on top of paper and lighting the fire. When he was done, they all sat down for dinner.*
>
> *No one paid attention when Jill roamed away from her chair and was approaching the fire with a sheet of newspaper in her hands. All of a sudden her mother, Connie, screamed, "Jill! No!" and dashed to catch the child just before she bent down to thrust the paper into the fire.*
>
> *Jill burst out crying. Connie was ready to reproach Jill for not following her father's instructions, but Jill's wails gave her time to reconsider her reaction. Instead of expressing anger at her child, she said, "I was so scared when I saw you near the fire with a paper in your hand. I was afraid you would burn yourself."*
>
> *"Paper in fire," Jill protested. She did not seem scared by her mom's abrupt move, but upset because her action was thwarted.*
>
> *Connie validated, "I know. Just as you were ready to put the paper in the fire, I got in your way. Did you want to see the fire get bigger?"*
>
> *Connie held Jill safely by the fire and Jill said, "Mom, you put the paper."*
>
> *Connie condensed the paper and put it in the fire carefully. She told Jill to stay away from the fire and to ask for Mom's or Dad's help if she wanted to make it bigger.*

As often as possible, grant your child the freedom to make her own decisions. However, when you must restrict her freedom, do so with respect and kindness and back your choice with an explanation. Even if your child's choice or inquiry is objectionable to you, if it is harmless, hold back your impulse to direct her. Use S.A.L.V.E.: Separate your personal reaction from what is going on for your child and examine your thoughts to see whether they are even relevant; give attention, listen, validate, empower, and give useful information. Your child has a right to go through her own trials and errors and to have feelings about it. For example, your three-year-old may need to find out for herself that she can't carry your suitcase, and your eleven-year old may have to discover independently that she cannot get a job at the supermarket, or at least verify your guess. If, when she finds out, she feels disappointed, listen and validate.

When a child arrives at answers on her own, she learns to face disappointments of which she is the cause and not the victim. There is no one to blame or to feel resentful toward. She is responsible for what happens to her, and she learns firsthand what does and does not work. When she can express the emotions that arise along the way with your loving attention, these experiences become valuable stepping stones on her path toward self-confidence and resourcefulness.

Distraction

Distraction is another strategy for avoiding or denying feelings. Offering candy or a fun activity to an upset child tells her to run away from her feelings. A scraped knee or a lost toy can evoke pain and sadness. The pain does not disappear by eating sweets or noticing something enchanting. The message the child is internalizing when distracted is that something is wrong with having feelings. "Mom doesn't want me to express my pain. I shouldn't feel or express pain. I am supposed to get busy quickly with something else. I should avoid all emotional discomfort and take no risks because falls are bad." This does not lead to happiness, but to weakness and an undaring existence. By distracting we convey to the child the idea that reality is bad and should be overcome; the underlying message is "Something is wrong." However, happiness lies in learning to live with reality and in solving problems not because of fear of what happens, but in freedom to make life more nurturing.

Distracting a child from emotions can also be one of the causes for later drug use, overuse of painkillers, and a tendency to always search for easy answers. It can breed adults who easily feel overwhelmed because their tolerance for difficulty is low. The commitment to avoid discomfort restricts their freedom to create full and vibrant lives.

A child can acquire resilience in the face of hurts and difficulties when she sees those as part of life. Therefore, when we notice a need to interrupt, fix, distract, or give advice, we can stop ourselves and explore the drive inside us. Although it may seem to us that we are driven by the desire to do the best for the child, most often we discover that the child is better off without our input.

Avoidance

Avoidance is pretending not to notice a child's unwanted expression in hope that it will go away. Parents hope that by giving no attention to the expression, it will not be "re-enforced" and will therefore diminish over time. The question always comes back to: Why do we want feelings and their expressions to go away? After all, what we want the most is to experience life emotionally; humanity devotes much time and resources to evoking strong feelings without which we feel listless and bored. In addition, your child's emotions bring up your own, offering you the opportunity to raise yourself; you learn about you (S of S.A.L.V.E.,) and the clarity you gain helps you learn about your child.

If you catch yourself using the avoidance approach, be patient and forgiving to yourself, and, at the same time, stop yourself from running on these old tracks laid for you by others. Sadly, a child whose painful feelings are being avoided will indeed diminish or stop expressing herself and may even stop feeling them, becoming emotionally numb and hard to connect with. Or, in the healthier child, she will escalate her communication by choosing provocative behaviors that may finally get our attention. In addition, when a parent uses avoidance, the child's needs will not be met, leading to more stress with its many difficult behavioral symptoms. A child's emotional outburst needs our caring response and attention to his needs (which is not necessarily what he wants at the moment, as we shall see later).

Inducing Fear

Inducing fear is another common strategy for shutting down a child's expression of feelings. Denial, avoidance, and distraction are enough to inhibit a child's self-expression, because she gets the message that when she is emotional, approval seems to vanish. If her rage, frustration, or tears meet with scolding, demeaning remarks, or punishment, her fear will most likely grow into insecurity and submissiveness or into active rage and aggression.

Granting a child emotional freedom means loving her when she mourns the loss of her cat, rages over a broken toy, or has a tantrum over choosing what clothes to wear. When we cherish her power to feel and to let go, she will accept those as natural. Investigate and heal your own fear of feelings so that your child can be safe to let it all out when she's around you. She will then develop the courage to feel and the capacity to move on.

Some people can let painful emotions pass through them and move on happily without expressing them. This is very different from suppressing feelings. Suppressing means that the pain is buried, while letting it pass through means that the person does not have a great attachment to the thoughts and their related feelings. If you are one who can let go of your feelings with ease without expressing them first, realize that most people, including children, cannot move on unless they express their feelings first with validating attention. Your ease, however, will help your child perceive her own emotions as passersby to experience and then move on.

Honoring feelings does not mean wallowing in them; on the contrary, when we can freely let go of our emotions, they pass through and leave us free to act effectively. Experiencing life fully in the present dissolves pain and allows us to move into the next present moment with clarity.

Crying

Humans are endowed with a great emotional capacity; to be able to manage intense feelings, we have been given the ability to cry. Children use crying naturally, and we must learn to understand their communication as well as to support their use of tears for healing. Responding to the crying of the baby is what teaches him that he has power over his own life, that he can trust us, and that he is important. As the baby grows into a toddler and a child, he uses words and gestures as well as tears.

Many parents have a hard time distinguishing emotional expressions in babies. Indeed, most of the time, a baby's cry is a communication about needs that have to be met. However, even for babies, there are times when the actual need is to cry.

> In one of my parenting classes, the question of crying babies came up. Teresa was beside herself with frustration about her baby's inconsolable crying.
> "I do everything to soothe him: I nurse him, I rock him, I play with him and make noises, I run the water and give him a bath.... But, when the evening comes he just cries and screams like a wounded soul and nothing calms him."
> After the session about this subject, Teresa decided to try and validate her baby's feelings.
> "First I tried all my tricks to soothe him, from the breast to the merry-go-round. Then I sat down with him in my arms and ceased all attempts to stop his crying.

"I did the Self-investigation about what was driving me and I realized that I was the one needing soothing because I told myself that my baby's crying meant that I am a bad mother and that something is wrong.

"When he takes short breaks, I usually hope that he is done crying. But then he resumes his wails. This time, when he took his first break, I said, 'Yes, I know, I know.' I didn't rock him. I didn't give him any hint that I expected him to stop crying and he went on. Every time he was silent I said something validating."

"Was his crying time any shorter?" asked another parent. (This parent was still looking for ways to stop the baby's crying.)

"No," she said. "On the contrary, once I let go of needing him to be happy, he cried more than usual, using my approval to its fullest. But, when he was done, instead of falling asleep exhausted, he was awake, alert, and happy. Later, when he did go to sleep, he did not cry and he woke up only once during the night and not the usual five to seven times."

Nate went on with his evening crying in his mother's loving arms for a couple of weeks. The periods of evening crying became gradually shorter until they ceased.

It is imperative to respond to a baby's cues. His cries are his communication. After all his needs are met, when no physical discomfort or illness is present and the baby is clearly not in need of something, we must respond to his need to cry. He might be crying because we are not getting what it is that he needs; still, if we have no clue, then he is left with frustration about which he needs to cry. We may guess what he feels as long as we realize that it is always a guess based on a projection of our own perception. Is he crying about the helplessness of being a baby? Missing the comfort of the womb? Wishing to speak to us and finding his tongue tied? Maybe he remembers the big face that hovered over him earlier and scared him...and so on.

When the need of the baby is unknown to us, we must validate his choice to feel the way he feels, let him know that his choice to wail is right, and that while he cries we are on his side, connected with love, affection, and understanding. Always hold your crying baby. Your inability to know why he cries does not change his need to be held at all times, and particularly when he is in distress. He must be successful in connecting with you and in getting you to act on his behalf or give him your full attention. The more a child succeeds in generating your care, the more he will find calm ways to communicate. Why have a fit if just a small cue or a word can get him the attention to his need?

When your baby is held on your body consistently, he is unlikely to cry for basic physical needs. Instead, he gives you subtle cues and you respond promptly so he has no need to use crying to communicate. Babies who are carried in arms and slept with rarely cry to alert you for a simple need. If a baby who is cared for in this manner cries, and he is not sick or injured, most likely he needs to cry.

As they grow up, children gradually use more words instead of cues or crying. However, they keep using tears to express physical and emotional pain for the rest of their lives. While adults can express pain that is not severe with words alone, children use tears easily and effectively.

As the child gets older, you will be able to know exactly what causes his hurt, so you will be able to validate his feelings with more accuracy. For example, you might say to a child who is crying because his plan is cancelled, "You waited so long to go to the park and it started to rain." Hold him while he cries until he is done and he lets you know that he is ready to move on. If he pushes you away, stay close, attentive, and available. Sometimes parents tell me that they want the child to be so happy that he has no need to cry. However, in our effort to raise children who don't cry, we may be denying a need that is as basic as love, food, and air. Like a river that was dammed, these tears will find other outlets through aggression, tics, sleep, food disorders, and other difficulties. Tears are here to stay, so we will benefit from embracing them rather than suppressing them. Powerful people are not those whose life flows with no pain, but those who have the strength to move *through* pain and come out richer on the other side.

The following example from my counseling work demonstrates the healing power of tears even for serious symptoms.

> *Seven-year-old Tony started hitting his older sister almost every day. His parents reported that in addition to his aggression, his usual cheerful spirit had been replaced with impatience and anger. They tried to meet Tony's need for more attention and to control his aggression by restricting and scolding. As a result, Tony reduced the hitting, but started chewing his shirt and blinking his eyes uncontrollably.*
>
> *When I asked Tony's parents whether he shows feelings of sadness or fear or if he cries, they realized that he had not shed tears in a long time. At the next session Tony's sister, Becky, said, "Tony's best friend made fun of him when he cried."*
>
> *"What does he do when he feels hurt?" I asked her.*

Becky thought for a moment and then said, "Oh, that's when he blinks his eyes to stop the tears."

I then played the game Truth or Dare with Tony. When truth was his choice I asked, "Do you sometimes feel sad when you don't get what you want?"

Being true to the game he responded positively.

"And do you try to hold your tears in, so no one would know?" I added.

"Yes," he said and nodded.

"I understand," I said. "Did you know that holding tears inside is like not going to the bathroom when you need to?"

Tony pondered over this startling statement. "Really?" he said, looking at me with his huge brown eyes. "What happens if you don't go to the bathroom?" he asked, then hurried to answer his own inquiry. "Well, you can't."

"Yes," I said. "You can't, so that your body will stay healthy."

"Will my tears make me ill when I hold them?"

"No," I said (although it could). "You can't stop them either. It only makes your feelings find a different way out."

"How?"

"How do your tears find a way out? What is it you do that you can't control?"

"Oh, you mean being angry and blinking my eyes?"

"Yes, those are some of your ways."

"Gee, I will cry from now on. That's better. I hate blinking my eyes."

Tony's parents reported that the next day Tony was disappointed with a gift he received and, with his mother's validation, sobbed in her arms for about fifteen minutes. The blinking has disappeared. Tony's parents found ways to empower his need for physical expression by enrolling him in a karate class, which he loved. The shirt-chewing lasted a while longer and then vanished as well. Although Tony still had a tendency to use his body to express anger, this became rare. His parents' validation and trust made it safe for him to feel and to be vulnerable. It was now easier to connect with him and he could express himself and cry when he needed to.

A child's symptoms or new variations of old ones can recur any time he is holding in his tears and feelings. When we know a child well, we can read his personal signals and make it safe for him to let out the accumulated anxiety.

We aim at preventing the accumulation of suppressed emotions; yet, often we see things clearly only after they get out of hand. This is part of our humanity, which a child is destined to live with. Therefore, when you find that you have been blind to a need of your child for a while, realize that this is often the normal course of events and move peacefully toward the next step of meeting the need and unleashing the sadness for both your child and yourself.

Separation Anxiety and the Need to Cry

At times, the notion of releasing pain through tears can be taken too far. When a friend once asked me why I was taking my toddler with me on a speaking engagement, I replied that if I left him, he would feel scared and desperate (in addition to needing to nurse). I should go anyway, my friend protested, since his father would be with him to validate his feelings and it would be good for him to cry, thereby releasing past hurts over abandonment.

My child had no past abandonment to cry about and I was not about to give him such an experience. Consequently, I took my son with me on the speaking engagement and on future trips as long as he needed. When he was ready to let me go, there were no tears; he initiated the separation and was peaceful about being apart from me. Trusting that all my child's emotional expressions represent real and urgent needs for closeness and safety, I simply fulfill them. Even if we know about a past pain that could use healing, as my friend suggested, there is no purpose in staging opportunities for a child to cry. If she feels safe to express herself, she will create the circumstances in which to vent old hurts. Later in this chapter you will find an example of a child "processing past hurts."

When circumstances make separation unavoidable (hospitalization or other calamities), then, and only then, being unable to avoid the separation, we give supportive attention to the child's fears and tears; we validate and empower the child in the face of life's circumstances, but we don't manufacture those events. In other words, offer validation to the crying child, but don't cause his tears.

When separation is unavoidable, our task is not to distract the child from her feelings, but rather to validate her experience so she can cry fully and recognize the validity of her experience. Likewise, upon returning from being away and facing a furious child, you need not attempt to stop her expression or to offer her a gift to placate her; you need only validate, show her you care, and express your own longing and love by mostly just holding and listening. Your child will recover from the agony of separation by crying and/or by expressing her fears and frustrations with your validating attention and love. Your unwavering support will pass on to her the message that she is perfectly capable of going through this experience.

Tantrums: Crying for a Need or a Need for Crying?

A child who throws a tantrum is feeling helpless and in need for autonomy and a sense of dignity. He must be able to generate his own life on his own terms. Sometimes a tantrum requires our attention to a specific issue; other times, the child needs to unleash intense emotions about that which is not changeable, and he needs our loving attention. When he heals himself through raging and we offer to soothe him and talk him out of his rage, we thwart his healing session; but, when we control the child, we cause the tantrum.

When you control your child and you cause his rage, do the self-talk investigation and search in your heart for who you want to be with your child. The kind and loving parent that you are does not want to control and aggravate your child. Your mind is saying something that drives your unproductive words or actions. What are your thoughts? "She should leave the playground when I tell her to…" Really? Would you follow anyone but your own heart when you are having a great time? Do you leave the party right away when your child is bored or your spouse asks to? Are these thoughts kind and honest? It is really your own inner tantrum that is expressed by your child. Your need to control is out of control and you may be torn between impressing someone and responding to your child. Ask yourself, how you would be with your child in the same situations if you didn't even have these thoughts? Just imagine yourself, free of the inner chatter in the same situation, and observe in your mind how you would treat your child.

Tantrums are not inevitable and preventing them starts with baby care and with an attitude of "yes" to the baby and then the child's direction. Hold the baby constantly, so he develops gentle communication skills. Slings and co-sleeping allow a baby or a toddler to give signals without crying and without feeling frustrated. He then develops the distinction between making requests peacefully and crying to express emotions. Later, as he acquires language, he is likely to go on and use words, not tantrums, to communicate his needs. When the child knows that his words elicit parental response, as did his gentle cues as a baby, he has no reason to scream for attention; therefore, if such a child throws a tantrum, he most likely needs your listening or your care to something that has gone wrong.

The confusion starts when the child throws a tantrum because his gentler communication did not produce the needed connection with you. This is not a reason to feel guilty or inadequate as a parent. It occurs for almost every child, in spite of parents' best intentions to be responsive and kind.

If you feel anxious when your child rages over that which is unchangeable, you might rush to give the screaming child anything, change reality, compensate, and even do things against all logic just to stop the tantrum. In this way you don't listen to his message and you thwart his healing session. Such a response gradually teaches the child to use tantrums and tears not for self-healing, but for getting things. There is no one to point the finger at for this misunderstanding. It is part of the human condition; both parent and child are caught in their own minds' strategies and doing their best. Parents may perceive that the child is "manipulating" them. Yet, he is only responding to the cues given to him with the best of intentions.

To avoid panic when your child rages over an unchangeable situation, use the self-talk of S.A.L.V.E.; investigate your thoughts rather than let them dictate your actions. Your thoughts are likely to be "I must make him happy," "What's wrong with him?", "I am such a bad parent," "What am I doing wrong?", "Oh no, the poor child, that's terrible," "If people see him they will think I don't know how to be a parent," and the likes. Write them down and look at your mind on paper.

These thoughts, when you believe them to be true, send you off on a crusade to fight the reality of your child's tantrum. While doing so, you are actually disconnected from your child and from yourself. When you investigate these thoughts, you find that they have nothing to do with truth, reality, or your child. They are simply anxieties you inherited as a human being. Without them you would have no problem loving your child unconditionally and giving him full attention.

When you investigate your thoughts, notice that they are all about you, naturally, because they are *your* thoughts. You are the one thinking that something is wrong, terrible, or that your image in the eyes of others is being harmed. You are the one with the desire to stop the tantrum for your own sake based on these thoughts. If you look deep inside, you don't even know that these thoughts are true for you. They are automatic. If you had a way to explore how you would react if these thoughts didn't occur to you, your child's tantrum may look completely harmless and you may respond with much more love and be connected to your child.

A tantrum is a valid way to express intense pent-up emotions and as such it is a process of healing. Crying or raging that is used to get the unattainable is easy to prevent by tuning up our responses to the child's peaceful cues and by avoiding coercion. When healing tantrums do occur and are stopped by compensations, the problem is left unresolved because the real need has not been addressed.

The Price of Controlling

When limitations are imposed on the child, she tends to oppose them and to harbor resentment, leading to tantrums or aggression. It can also lead to compliance, which parents often mistake for being a "good" child. The compliant child is likely to show her accumulated distress through other emotional disturbances or later in her teens or adult life with the use of drugs, aggression, eating disorders, depression, and other difficulties.

Helplessness is the key emotion behind rage. We can prevent a child's helplessness by not taking away her power and by protecting her freedom of choice and self-governing. At the same time, we must avoid burdening her with power beyond her ability to handle, which is often power over others. The combination of helplessness on the one hand and excess power on the other overwhelms a child.

There are situations in which our experience is useful to the child for her safety and well-being. Yet, although there are rare times when we may need to act fast and explain afterwards, in most of life's circumstances this is not necessary. Instead, when a child is about to do something unsafe or inconsiderate, give her information that she can use to make safe and considerate choices. In this way you avoid the need to act with interventions, limits, and controls that insult her and put you above her.

A child feels powerful when she makes autonomous choices and owns her decisions. However, having autonomy is very different than having control over others, which is scary for a child. If you panic in the face of your child's emotions she will use her power over you, but having such power overwhelms her and leads to more tantrums.

If most of the time a child is given information so she can make autonomous choices, she will be able to accept situations in which she cannot do whatever she wishes: She cannot ride her tricycle in the middle of the street, break dishes, play with fire, hurt others, hurl objects in the house, or ride in the car without a seat belt. When these realizations are based on constructive communication rather than on control, the child's natural desire to make the right choices is likely to lead her to doing what is considerate and safe because that is what she wants.

By nature children yearn to do the right things, fit in, be safe, and please us. If your child resists you, it is a sign that you have exercised control in relating to her; you have been resisting her. Whatever you judge in your child is likely to be a useful guide for yourself, so use it for your own growth and your child will improve because you do; she is only mirroring your attitudes. If you see her as resisting, you must be resisting. If she is uncooperative ask yourself how cooperative you are with her. Write down and investigate the thoughts that fuel your need to control; when you shed light on these automatic responses they gradually let you be the parent you love being.

The following are two examples from workshops I led that illustrate ways of dealing with one safety problem in two different ways, one with control and the other with trust and human connection:

> *Amber's father told her to never play by the creek that goes through their yard without her parents being there with her. Two weeks later, Amber, who is three-years-old, thought she would just get a little closer to the water and throw a stone in. As she did so, she was startled by her mother's yell: "No, Amber! Get away from there right now!"*
>
> *Amber retreated, scared and ashamed. Her mother kept scolding her and threatened to punish her next time.*

It is possible that Amber will not go to the creek by herself again, but not because she understands, not because she trusts her parents, and not because of trusting herself and wishing to stay safe. If she avoids the creek it is out of fear of parental disapproval and punishment. If she is enraged one day and desires revenge, she might take a chance and "punish" her parents by going into the creek or taking some other "forbidden" steps. Or, when she does not want their approval, but rather wishes to experience her own autonomy, she may satisfy that desire by doing whatever is "forbidden." One way or another she is likely to have many other oppressive experiences with her parents and a lot of anger to express through tantrums, aggression, or self-destructiveness.

A child will want to stay safe and take care of herself when given information and when feeling safe with her parents. She feels safe when her parents are not enforcing rules, but rather being her loving allies.

> *Julian's father asked him if he would like to play by the creek that ran by their new house, and he did. They went together to the creek and Father explained to three-year-old Julian about the danger of water. Julian's father demonstrated by throwing leaves and stones into the stream, and explained how people cannot breathe if they fall in the water. Then they put their feet in and felt the velocity of the stream. After playing and having a lot of fun, he requested of Julian to always ask him or his mother to go with him when he wanted to play by the creek.*
>
> *The next day Julian asked his mother to go with him to the creek. "I cannot go at this minute," Mom said. "But as soon as I am through with this phone call, I will." Twenty minutes later mother and son went to the creek. After a period of almost daily creek adventures, Julian lost the initial interest and his creek play with Mom or Dad became random. He never went there by himself because he trusted his parents and his own sense, which he acquired in their presence.*

With a relationship of trust as we see in the second example, Julian has no reason to feel helpless, as he is not being controlled. Nor does he develop a desire to defy his parents. He will keep using his parents' information over the years in all areas of life with little desire to breech agreements or do anything unsafe or inconsiderate.

Whenever possible, give information and avoid putting the child in situations too difficult for him to understand and make a safe choice. Providing a safe physical and social environment makes it possible for a child to take safe and considerate actions.

When a Child Uses a Tantrum to Get What He Wants

A child who uses emotional expression as a way to get something is assuming two things based on his experience: he cannot get it any other way and, if he screams loud enough, and long enough he will get what he wants or some other compensation. The result is two unsettling states of mind: He feels helpless due to parental control on the one hand and overwhelmed by too much power when his tears make his parents panic.

While feelings are always valid, they are not necessarily a basis for action. A child who is upset because he was asked to stop throwing sand on another child, or a child who is disappointed because he didn't get to be first in line both have valid feelings that they need to express, to be listened to, and to be validated. It doesn't mean we encourage a child to throw sand on people or that we fight for his right to be first. (We do, however, need to find out if there is some unmet need that drives the child's intentions.)

Your youngster may be furious that you wouldn't push the other child out of his way so he could be first or that he could not keep throwing sand at a younger child in the park. If he has experienced a lot of helplessness and the lack of freedom to govern his own life, this upset may bring up a tantrum. Likewise, if he often feels overwhelmed by his power over you or by license to do as he wishes, he is likely to go into rage in order to elicit your leadership.

As much as we wish to avoid controlling, there are situations when intervention is a must and there is no time for a conversation. The child is then likely to feel hurt, dismayed, or enraged. Here is an example that illustrates the freedom a child gains when her wails don't change reality but are listened to and validated:

> Five-year-old Dave asked to be with his older sister Lila, who is nine, in her room. Lila wanted to be by herself. Dave pleaded and Lila agreed with a condition that Dave would not push her the way he was doing earlier. Dave promised.
>
> After a short while Dave came out, crying. "Lila told me to leave because I pushed her."
>
> As it turned out Lila gave her brother a few opportunities to stop pushing before she asked him to leave.
>
> Dave threw himself on the floor next to his mother and screamed that he wouldn't push his sister again and that he wanted to go back.
>
> His mother validated his feelings. "You wanted to play with your sister. You couldn't help yourself and pushed her. Did you want her to wrestle with you?"
>
> "I want to go back," Dave cried and kicked.
>
> Mom said, "I understand. I will be with you here so you can cry as much as you need."
>
> Dave stopped the tantrum immediately and went to ride his tricycle.

Dave did not need to cry but was hoping to change reality. When he found out that it wasn't going to happen, he went on to another activity. When a child's goal is to get something by throwing a tantrum, the information about giving attention to his crying brings the tantrum to an end because it is useless as a tool.

While throwing a tantrum to get the impossible, a child may still need to express his emotions. Our job in such situations is to listen and acknowledge, until the tantrum comes to its natural end. Most often the child will then be content and need nothing; but if there is still a need, the discussion can begin after the storm is over.

What the child wants at the time is often not the actual need; as parents we must look for the drive behind the tantrum, which is usually something larger than a candy or being first. For example, a tantrum over wanting to be first may signify needing to feel secure and having a sense of being important and valued. Coercing his friends to let him be first won't solve the deeper problem but actually feed it further. The underlying need has to be addressed or else more tantrums will ensue, fed by more insecurity. If all the child needs is to express rage, he will need nothing once he is done. On the other hand, if he needs love, attention, or autonomy, when he fully expresses his rage, both he and you will gain clarity and see practical solutions as the following story demonstrates:

> Four-year-old Sheila left home with her parents to visit Uncle John in the hospital. The ride was a couple of hours long, and by the time they got to the hospital Sheila was sound asleep. Considering how tired Sheila was, her parents did not wake her up. Her father stayed with her in the car while her mom went to visit her brother. When the short visit ended, Sheila was still asleep.
>
> When Sheila woke up, it was dark and they were almost at home. Sheila looked around:

"How much longer before we get to Uncle John?"
she asked.

Her parents informed her that they were almost back home and Sheila exploded with a tantrum. Her parents suggested another trip the following weekend, but solutions were not what Sheila needed at the moment. "No, I wanted to see him now!" Sheila screamed while kicking violently. She went on with the tantrum for the rest of the ride with her mother's full attention and care. Mom acknowledged the facts and validated Sheila's feelings. "You were excited to visit Uncle John, and then you missed it. You wanted to choose whether you kept sleeping or were woken up."

After she was done with her tantrum, Sheila seemed calm. They came home and discussed ways to include her in future decisions and honor her need for self-governing. The family planned another visit to Uncle John the following weekend, which, now that she was calm, Sheila was looking forward to. They all agreed that before each trip, Sheila would announce in advance her choice to be woken up or not, in case they arrive somewhere while she sleeps. If she forgets to announce, she will be awakened by default.

Such situations are perplexing for parents and many would have come up with creative ways to stop the tantrum: Could they have gone back that night and stayed in a motel to return the next day? Offered to go out for a yummy treat on the way home? Buy a new toy?

The intent behind such solutions is to stop the child's tantrum so we can spare ourselves the unpleasant story about it. We tell ourselves that the child is traumatized, that we are guilty, and that the child can't handle the disappointment. Yet, what happened is not reversible. The parents are not guilty but innocent in doing their best, and the child is not trauma-tized unless we teach her that she is. Such solutions would not have taken care of Sheila's needs and feelings anyway. It is not the missed visit that carried the sharpest part of her anger, but the disregard for her autonomous right to make her own deci-sions about herself. No visit, ice cream, or playground can give her back her dignity. On the other hand, listening, acknowl-edging reality, and validating the rage she freely expressed enabled Sheila to move through her intense feelings and con-sider future solutions. Being only four, she did not even need to investigate her thoughts to realize that the source of her rage was wishing the impossible. The drama vanished just by let-ting it move through. Without her drama about what she missed, she can look forward to next week.

Listen to your child's tantrum and acknowledge what hap-pened, but don't save or distract him from feelings. He needs to know that there is no need to panic and no need to find a quick compensation to stop the pain when things go wrong. He needs to experience himself as emotionally capable of having strong feelings and of facing disappointments, falls, or others hurts.

Parental Leadership

As with crying, some parents may take the idea of a tan-trum as self-healing to an extreme and deny a child her needs and autonomy. Instead of honoring her choices, they may say, "Let her rage, it's good for her." Respect the child's need to rage, but don't cause it. It is fine to replace a broken banana if available or to offer a healthy candy without a power struggle. Allow yourself to be kind, generous, and respectful.

A father said to me, "But if I succumb, she won't respect me." Being kind is not about "succumbing." The parent's need to be "respected" is another one of these thoughts that can use a deep investigation. Raising ourselves is the part where we become free of needing anything that another should give us. Respect yourself and others and you will be a teacher of respect.

A child's authentic sense of respect develops through the experience of love and kindness, not control. We often mistake submissiveness for respect. Yet obedience is not respect but another manifestation of fear mingled with resentment, and therefore leads to the same shutdown of self-expression. A parent's fear of being exploited by the child is most often the result of personal, past-related pain. It has nothing to do with the child and it gets in the way of loving and trusting her. The child who is listened to and whose life flows unhindered by an adult's control has no need to use her parents. She feels love and admiration for them and she trusts them to be on her side.

When children feel helpless and use tantrums as a tool to get things, they are asking for your leadership. They need freedom and autonomy, but they don't want to believe they can scare their parents with their emotional expression. They are unequipped to handle this kind of power and therefore when a child finds that her parent is scared of her crying or screaming, she feels lost and in need of guidance. A child needs parents to be leaders she can lean on, and listeners into whose ears she can pour her heart. In other words, your child is counting on your strength to absorb her feelings without being overwhelmed.

To prevent the use of tantrums as a tool to get things, *you must alter the two conditions that give rise to a child's rage:*

1) Let go of control; make it possible for your child to direct her life peacefully and autonomously.
2) When she is upset about that which is unchangeable, validate your child's feelings without giving her emotional expression the power to alter reality.

When facing disappointments and frustration, children rely on parental leadership. Their unspoken question is often something like this: "Will my daddy love me enough to listen to my rage or is he going to give up on me in the face of my intense feelings and try to stop me?" In effect, your youngsters need to feel safe to go "nuts" and know that you have the strength to hold a loving space for them.

If you panic in response to a child's tantrum, she learns not only to use it as a tool, but also to fear emotions and to take them too seriously. She may become scared to feel her own emotions, because she sees that you can't handle feelings either: "Feelings must be horrible; I must avoid them." This whole dramatic reaction to feelings also gives them exaggerated significance and they become scary and potent. In contrast, when we validate feelings in a calm spirit, without adding drama, they can be experienced with confidence. Feelings are here to pass through us, so we can move on free of their grip. It is resisting and negating that causes the real anguish.

Compensation and distraction don't help a child pass through her emotions. If she wants to have a healing tantrum, she will not be satisfied with getting what she asked for; she will come up with other reasons for upset or she may ask for the impossible. Even if an expression of rage is successfully stopped, the child will resume her fit in her own creative ways, usually within the same day. When we say, "No matter what I give her, she keeps coming up with upsets," we are most likely describing a child who needs to express intense feelings. Doing acrobatics to give her whatever she screams for actually thwarts her real intent, and it prevents you from knowing the underlying cause of her distress.

Use the S.A.L.V.E. formula and the unmet needs will present themselves clearly:

S - Separate yourself and investigate your own inner voice which tells you to stop the child's tantrum; listen Silently to your own Self-talk. If you can let it be, move on. If you cannot, investigate it for relevance. If you have a thought, "My child should stop raging" or "She can't handle such frustration," ask yourself if you can really know that. Then imagine being with your raging child without that thought. You may discover peaceful clarity that may surprise you. Notice that the stressful thought you have about your child, represents you just as well or better; you are having an inner tantrum over your child's tantrum. Meanwhile, your child needs your listening and your calm leadership.

A - Once you generate some clarity inside of you, put your Attention on the child.

L - Listen to her rage.

V - Validate her feelings.

E - Empower her to unleash her emotions and to resolve her issue.

When you hear your child fully, you will stay connected, be relaxed, and be able to detect her real need, as did Sheila's parents in the earlier example (page 134). If Sheila's mother hadn't listened, she would have been caught in her own remorse and maybe driven back to the hospital or compensated Sheila some other way. Instead, she did listen to Sheila and saw that her need was to govern her own choices and to be included.

To notice the child without our drama clouding our vision, we must learn to listen with awareness that goes beyond mere words. "I wanted to visit my uncle" may look like the most important need, but the deeper hurt comes from having no say and from not being included. Most rage reflects the need for freedom to self-govern. Sheila can accept the loss of that day's visit when her need for autonomy and inclusion is heard. Trust your child and respect her need to cry without confusing it with a cry for another need.

Preventing the "Victim" Psychology

Children who repeatedly get compensated for crying and appearing miserable learn another lesson: "With enough anguish, I can get what I want" or "Being miserable makes people pay attention." Many of us who have learned this strategy in childhood carry it on into our adult relationships, telling ourselves, "If I prove how miserable I am, he/she will treat me nicely or do what I want."

Self-victimizing children and adults end up falling into bad circumstances in the unconscious belief that this will get them what they want. Eliciting pity is based on one's past and on giving the power to outside forces; it prevents us from being present and powerful. Your child learns from you to either be a victim or to be here now, able to act on his own behalf powerfully. If he learns that his happiness depends on others or on circumstances, he is helpless; there is nothing he can do about it. Victims have to keep falling because their mind wants to be right about their victim story.

When you find yourself caught in your own discomfort around your raging self-victimizing child, remind yourself that he relies on your leadership. He does not want you to get caught in his drama; that would be like joining a drowning person rather than pulling him out of the water. He counts on you to provide the clearing for his powerful (non-victim) self to emerge. The following example from a workshop participant illustrates the dangers of forfeiting parental leadership when a child is upset.

> *A few days before her sixth birthday, Nina discovered that her eleven-year-old brother, Ron, had a present for her. Ron planned to surprise her with the gift at her birthday party, but Nina didn't want to wait. She began to scream and cry that she wanted the present now. As Nina's screams filled the house, her father, Jack, felt irritated. He rushed into Ron's room and told him to give his sister her birthday present immediately.*
>
> *Ron fetched the gift and, in a fit of anger, threw it at his sister. At that point Nina stopped crying and Ron went back into his room and slammed the door.*

Nina's emotional outburst caused Jack to lose self-control. In his haste to stop the screaming, he failed to provide the leadership and the emotional support both his children needed. He disrespected his son's choice to give Nina her gift at the party, thereby depriving him of the pleasure of giving the gift when he wanted to. Jack also left his daughter with a power she couldn't handle, and no one to catch her in her emotional fall. What Nina needed instead was her father's understanding about her impatience so she could then embrace the moment as is. Furthermore, both children learned that misery and screaming is the ticket to getting one's way.

Innocently doing his best, Jack's intervention took care of no one but himself, and not without a price. He needed quiet, and he was as impatient as his daughter. He too wanted the "gift" right away; the "gift" he wanted was the end of the screaming. He was victimized by the screaming and his peace was dependent on his son's surrender to another victim. Innocently, every participant in this scene was a victim, and so no one gained real peace.

What might have been a more effective parental response? First, Jack could have refrained from involving himself in his children's argument; he could have noticed his own mind's conversation and realized it was about his own anxiety and confusion. Ron would not have given Nina her gift before her birthday party, and the screaming would have eventually played itself out, or Nina would have come to him with her story. Second, Jack could have offered to listen to Nina's anger and agitation and validate her feelings by saying, "I understand. You just can't wait to see the gift from your brother. Two days seem so long when you are excited about something." In addition to validating Nina's eagerness to open her gift, he could have shown that he cared about Ron's predicament by validating his feelings and preference. Then Nina would have felt understood and empowered to handle her own intense emotions, while Ron would have felt his father's trust and appreciation. Nina could have even investigated the source of her upset, which was her thinking that she should have the gift right away. Without that thought she would have been excited about another surprise awaiting her.

What if Nina had screamed for hours? Zen Buddhism has a helpful answer: So she cries and screams for a long, long time amid the loving attention of her father. Children sometimes cling to feeling upset because they need to cry; at other times they may be subconsciously pushing their parents into taking sides or into taking a strong position of leadership. There are also situations in which a child is simply a mirror of the parent or of the parents' relationship with each other. Regardless of what unconsciously drives the tantrum, validating emotions brings relief and clarity.

One useful guideline is not to alter the course of events unless they have the potential to be harmful or when a kind adjustment is called for. The reality in Jack's home was that Ron was going to give Nina her gift at the party. Empowering a child to come to terms with reality is a far greater gift than teaching her that if she is miserable and loud enough, reality will shape itself for her. Life does not provide reality shifts to fulfill human desires, and by omnipotently altering unwanted circumstances, we end up removing challenge and disappointment from the path of a child who would otherwise draw strength from them. In other words, the lesson of altering reality for a child is "You are too weak to be able to handle this" and "Something is wrong and must be changed." It is the point of view of the victim. In contrast, the lesson of focused listening says, "I trust you. You have the strength to go through this difficulty as well as to accept or resolve it." Your child then learns to love life rather than fear its many unexpected turns.

As long as a child's autonomy is respected, he will have the emotional capacity to withstand disappointments and to cope with occasional obstructions to his will. Children who have been taught to get things via emotional expression experience great relief when parents finally listen to their anguish.

Listening to Children's Anger

Anger is a feeling that expresses blame and causes one to focus outside of the self and away from her intimate thoughts and feelings. It is the result of seeing oneself as a victim. A child may rage about a lost toy, the rain that thwarted her play, or losing in a competitive game. In pointing a finger at someone or something, she renders herself powerless, because she can't change the past nor control other people; in essence she declares that her happiness depends on forces outside of herself and there is nothing she can do about it. Focusing outside prevents her from being inside and noticing the feelings that she does have power over.

An angry child will focus on how bad you are that you were late to give her a ride, and avoid the sadness about her missing a good chunk of the volleyball game. Yet, facing the loss of part of the game is a lot less painful than the hopelessness of wanting to go back in time and of controlling Dad's actions. Indeed, the truth in the moment is much kinder than the blame drama the mind adds to it. As you can see in the story in Chapter One (page 1) about Lizzie who missed her TV show, Lizzie made peace with staying in the store and missing the TV show as soon as she shifted from anger (blaming her mom and focusing on what was wrong) to being present to her loss: "So I missed the show." The reality wasn't as bad as her story about it, and she was easily able to make peace with it.

To assist your angry child, ask her questions that will help her realize the thoughts that lead to her anger and will connect her to those feelings that are not associated with blame. These painful thoughts are usually negations of reality, like "It shouldn't be this way" or "He shouldn't have broken my stick," or wanting the impossible: "I want to go home" (when you don't have the car and depend on a ride), "I want to be first," etc.

Ask your angry child questions that will help her connect with herself and focus on the thoughts and feelings that are not associated with blame. For instance, if your angry child blames, "They gave us a ride too early," you can validate the unspoken feeling: "Are you disappointed because you wanted to stay longer in the park?" Or if your child blames her sibling for having to go to the soccer practice, you can say, "Are you frustrated because you wish to go to the library and not to your brother's soccer practice?" If your child reacts to emotional words by feeling patronized and closing up, don't use those words. Just describe what occurred and what the child wanted: "Did you wish to stay longer in the park?" and "Oh, I see, you wanted to go to the library and not to the soccer game. I understand." Then listen to the child's own ways of describing her experience and don't negate her.

As soon as children shift their attention to whatever is present in their body and feelings, they often accept reality effortlessly; or, if not, they seem creative in coming up with or responding to productive solutions.

One of the reasons we often try to appease an angry child and stop her emotional expression is because we envision that listening to her will take too long. In reality, it only takes a long time when no relief is felt. Blaming gives no relief no matter how right the child is, and validation of blame only ignites it further. The focus on powers outside the self leaves a person helpless; the more she rages the more she digs herself emotionally in the painful hole of the helpless victim.

Keep in mind that we are dealing with situations that are aready over (scraped knee, grandma didn't come) or that we don't have control over. We can't stop the rain for our children and it wouldn't be good for them if we could. We also cannot change people, and so helping a child own her feelings will better prepare her to relate; she won't spend her life trying to change people to fit her expectations. Instead she will learn to live with people and make choices that don't assume controlling them in any way.

To bring about self-realization, ask questions that may assist your child in discovering the thoughts, meanings, and fears that cause her anger. Useful questions are those that help the child see herself as the cause of her feelings (not of what happened). Once she is aware of her own thought process and in touch with the feelings that result from it, she can gain clarity (as well as provide clarity for you) towards productive solutions.

You can use one of these four basic questions designed to explore the thoughts that cause anger and other painful emotions:

> *"What do you think it means?"*
> *"How would it be if you had it your way?"*
> *"What's the worst that can happen?"*
> *"How should it be?"*

Even a very young child can gain clarity by looking at the way she speaks to herself that causes her anger. You may need to be more specific with the young:

> *"Did you think that if he calls you 'stupid' you really are?"*
> *"How would you be if he didn't call you 'stupid' right now?"*
> *"What's the worse that can happen now?"*
> *"Do you think that he shouldn't call you 'stupid'?"*

Once the child is looking at the thoughts that cause the pain, you can ask how she would be in the same situation without her ideas about it. She can then see how the cause of her anger is not what happened, but her thoughts about it. What happened, even when unwanted, is much easier to live with than the fearful or painful thoughts the mind comes up with. Without the blame and drama, she is no longer dependent on anyone else to give her happiness and is likely to tap into her own power. When reality is unyielding, clinging to painful thoughts of wanting the impossible causes suffering. Children are fast to realize this, unless we teach them that clinging to pain reaps benefits that are worth the trouble.

The following example shows how the question "What does it mean to you?" can assist a child in recognizing his deeper emotions and their cause. When his mother helps him to investigate the validity of his thoughts, he discovers that the meaning he added caused his pain and his helplessness:

> *Twelve-year-old Mario was outraged about his younger brothers.* He told his mother Beth, a single parent, they were constantly disturbing him and he felt enraged that they never had to deal with consequences for their behavior. Beth asked, "Do you want me to prevent your brothers from annoying you?"
>
> "I suppose so," he started, then went on with as much anger, "Do something, I don't know. You just never do anything. They are such a pain."
>
> Beth noticed that Mario's focus was on blame, revenge, and punishment, and that her question was not helpful because she implied that a solution depended on what she should do to his brothers rather than on his own self-realization about his relationship with his brothers.
>
> "Do you think that it means that I don't care?" she asked. (This is the first of the four helpful questions.)
>
> "Yes. And that you don't love me."
>
> "Oh dear, that hurts," she said. "Do you really think that I don't care about you when I don't intervene?" (Checking validity.)
>
> "No. I know that you care."
>
> "How would you feel if you weren't thinking that I didn't care?" (Detecting the added meaning as the cause of pain.)
>
> "Oh, I don't know. They are still annoying, but then I can actually handle it by myself."
>
> "So what is hurting most is the thought that I don't care?"

"Hmm, yes, I guess so," Mario said and started to cry. Then without any prompting he started laughing and said, "Well, I do know that you love me." Beth hugged him.

"I annoy them too," Mario went on. "I guess I just need time away from them. And, when they annoy me, I can be the one taking care of myself."

That evening they had a family meeting and discussed ways to solve sibling disputes and to respect Mario's need for privacy. After they came up with some suggestions, Mario said, "Let's drop it. I can handle my relationship with you guys. I was just caught in this silly idea that Mom doesn't care."

The actual story is rarely the real issue. Mario created anger by telling himself that his mom's lack of intervention on his behalf meant that she didn't care about him. His anger had nothing to do with his brothers. As long as he was attached to his interpretation that his mother didn't care or love him, Mario had to fail in resolving things with his brothers; if he handled his relationship with them, his "story" about his mother would be destroyed. Once Mario took responsibility for the meaning he invented, he had no problem resolving issues with his brothers. Beth told me later that she had her own awakening about expressing love. She realized that she wasn't spending much time with Mario and she resolved to spend more one-on-one time with him.

Shifting from blame to self-realization does not mean that we don't take action to aleviate hurts when needed. On the contrary, clarity leads to productive solutions. For example, if a child is angry because she hates her new dance class, she may need to take action. When she is clear about what it is that is painful, she will know whether she should quit the class or look for another solution like switching her spot at the bar or communicating with the teacher. Instead of taking the challenge out of her hands, let her use it as grist for the mill for her own self-awareness and assertive action. With clarity, you too will learn a lot and you will know whether or not there is something you must do.

Avoid saying something that may invalidate your child's anger, such as "You're overreacting" or "Why are you so upset? It's no big deal." A child whose anger is invalidated will internalize the negative self-image and could become increasingly resentful and insecure. But mostly she will become even more defensive and unable to see positive solutions. In the story above, if Beth had invalidated Mario, she would have seemed to him even more uncaring, and he would have become even more devoted to his view that she didn't care.

To be with an angry child in a way that empowers her self-discovery, you must put your own reaction on hold and avoid trying to fix or control your child. Your ability to let go of control is a model of strength because you don't succumb to your mind's reaction; instead, you focus on your child, you move from reaction to creation and from weakness to power. True strength is not forceful, but tender.

Processing Past Hurts

At times children, like adults, need to retrieve past events to release their painful grip on them. When a child's past pain gets restimulated by a present occurrence, he will unleash the old pain with the new, often without realizing it. Youngsters may be unaware of how a present upset relates to a past event, or they may be the conscious designers of their own therapy. Children are ingenious at creating settings that allow them to express their emotions when they have the attention of a loving listener, as the following story demonstrates:

> *Michelle and I were talking in her living room while her son, seven-year-old Billy, and her daughter, three-year-old Thea, were playing outside. All of a sudden, we heard Thea scream. As Michelle and I stepped outside to see what had happened, we saw Thea's tricycle on its side in the grass. Then Billy announced that he had thrown his sister's bike on the ground.*
>
> *Michelle became angry and scolded, "Since when do you think you can throw bikes around?"*
>
> *"But you did it," Billy shouted.*
>
> *"That doesn't mean you can do it," Michelle yelled back.*
>
> *I was fascinated by Billy's clever retrieval of a bothersome past event so he could resolve it. After Michelle gave me permission to support her in responding to her son's spontaneous therapy session, I laid a calming hand on her shoulder and reminded her, "Whatever this is, it's about Billy."*
>
> *Billy then put his cards on the table. "On our trip to Minnesota, you threw my bike on the ground, and it broke," he said, looking at his mother and beginning to cry.*
>
> *Michelle validated Billy's rage, saying, "I threw your bike down. I see that you feel sad and angry. You want respect for what is yours."*
>
> *Billy went on, "You were mad at Grandpa, and because of that you threw my bike. That's not fair!"*

Welcoming her son's torrent of stored-up emotions about this episode, Michelle listened and presented no resistance. "You are right," she said, "I was not being fair. I expressed my rage by throwing your bike," whereupon Billy threw himself onto the grass and sobbed. Then almost as suddenly as he had started, Billy finished his "therapy session" by saying, "Okay, we can go to the park now," our planned agenda for the afternoon.

Billy didn't even need to explore his anger because he shifted into the non-blame feelings (sadness and tears) on his own as soon as he found no resistance from his mother. Children often move quickly when we flow with and not against their thinking. Many children's expressions, actions, and behaviors are their ongoing maintenance of emotional equilibrium. Unlike this story, in most situations we have no way of recognizing what the child is recreating. Whether in play, at the dinner table, at bedtime, or in the park, the thriving child leads his own way to an emotional clearing. He is generally content precisely because he is autonomous and because he is free to let his hurts out of his system.

The Parent's Self-Expression

Children are naturally self-expressive and have no desire to hide their feelings. To nurture this natural trait you must model by sharing your own emotions. Being vulnerable connects us to our children, while putting on a tough front separates us from them and teaches them isolation and mistrust.

Some parents fear that their emotions will hurt their children. However, you can avoid hurting others with your words without hiding your emotions. We hurt others when we burden them with the responsibility for our feelings or when we order them around and then get angry when they don't comply.

Speak as the author of your emotions and your preferences, and your words will hurt no one. When the children leave the dinner table a mess, and you say, "I feel like a slave in this house" or "I feel unappreciated," your child is likely to react with defiance and upset; these words blame and lay guilt as though it is up to the child to cater to your emotional needs. Yet, if you say, "I don't enjoy cleaning up after dinner by myself. I would like to have some participation with it," you blame no one, and you ask for what you want. When your child is not feeling responsible for your feelings, he will not be hurt by your expression. Make sure not to cloak your need in moralizing: "You should be helpful" or "You must learn to do your share" are not honest communications. Speak honestly: "I need your help. Will you be willing to clean up the table?"

After such communication, respect your child's autonomous choice of action or inaction. It is not her duty to meet your needs even when you are serving her. You want it cleaned. She doesn't care. She must feel safe to choose, without fear of your reaction or an obligation to please you, but by acting from an authentic desire that brings her joy and satisfaction. When her choice conflicts with your expectations, treat her with dignity and discuss her and your preferences until the two of you come to a solution that honors both of you. Generally speaking, having expectations gets in the way of embracing the flow of life as it comes and loving your child unconditionally. Your relationship with your spouse, your children, and others will flourish when you say "yes" to what is. More important, if your child chooses not to help you, he provides you with an opportunity to learn more about your own painful thoughts. When you think, "He should help" and he doesn't, you can use the teaching and find the freedom from this moral inside yourself. Who would you be without that expectation?

Parents often protest when they hear these suggestions and say, "But he has to get ready to go" or "He must go to sleep at bedtime" and "I really can't do it all by myself" and other examples that seem unavoidable. If you express yourself in a way that leaves the child emotionally free, he can be your partner, not your compliant subject. In turn you will discover that much of what you perceive as a "must" can be changed. You may be able to do your errands when your spouse is at home with the children or you can make the outing fun for the child; you can find working solutions to bedtime, meal-time, chores, and other sources of conflict. Sometimes doing things yourself takes less time and is much more peaceful. You are more likely to teach peace and participation when you express yourself authentically, and the only person you can be authentic about is you.

Express *your* self, not *your child's* self. The moment you blame, moralize, or give commands, you lose the connection with your child. When you expect compliance, your child resists; but, when you take care of you, your child can hear you and make choices about herself. You can then respect her choices because you are playing your role, not hers.

A child's ability to respond to your need is directly related to the way you express yourself. If you imply that your child is responsible for your feelings, she will be overwhelmed and intimidated, so much so that she is likely to be paralyzed by this burden and unable to relate to your expectations. Typical phrases that put responsibility for one's feeling on the child are:

- You make me feel...
- I feel unappreciated.
- You make me angry.
- You frustrate me.
- I can't handle your...
- When you are so noisy, I get a headache.
- You are driving me nuts.
- You are more than I can handle.
- I am exhausted already, you never stop...

We can also lay guilt without words or in more subtle ways with our facial expressions and body language. Develop your own list by becoming aware of phrases and expressions you use that elicit guilt. Being aware of the phrases that get you into the blame mode will help you resist using them.

Sometimes parents wish to protect a child from their more intense emotions. Yet, telling your child that you "feel fine" when you are obviously ready to explode teaches him to suppress or hide strong emotions and fear them. In addition, left to imagine why you are upset, your child, being self-centered by nature, is likely to either assume it is because of him, conclude that one has to be dishonest when feeling bad, or come up with some other life-draining interpretations.

If you are able to be present with your child without bringing up your personal distress, you need not necessarily bring it up. However, if you must express yourself, share your feelings in a safe way. You don't need to scare her with unnecessary details nor use her as your counselor. You can, however, share your feelings and any details that your child can safely include in her thoughts.

Make sure to talk about your feelings, not about blaming anyone or complaining. For example, if you arrive home ready to blow up, you can say, "I feel furious right now about something that happened at the bank. I need to scream." Or, learning of a friend's illness, you may say, "My friend, Tova, is very ill. I feel scared. I need time by myself and a session with my counselor." Sometimes you may want to add, "This has nothing to do with you. I will take care of it myself." Such simple explanations prevent the child from harboring guilt. Often, since she feels safe, she will show interest and care.

It is crucial that you recognize your own need for releasing intense emotions. If you have a spouse or a friend who can give you time and attention, arrange to have such time. If you need to make an appointment with a counselor, do so and let your bewildered child know that you are going to talk about your deep feelings with the counselor or that you will work on it yourself. If you do it yourself, follow the guidelines of self-investigating outlined in Chapter One.

It is not only the way you relate to your child that models ways of self-expression. Your interaction with your spouse and with other adults and children are a constant modeling for him. Learn to reveal the tenderness and depth of your feelings without hurting anyone. Seeing us cry, grapple with ambivalence, and give voice to other difficult emotions, children will retain their inborn freedom to express their own intense feelings and gain emotional strength and freedom.

You need not protect your child from your strong feelings, only avoid linking those with judgment of him or others. If you judge or blame, acknowledge your error and make amends. The only feelings not to be shared with a child are parental anxieties that would scare him in terms of his own or a family member's safety, like "I am scared that he'll get hurt," a thought that may hurt his self-perception, "I worry that he won't succeed," and your worries about his well-being, "He gets sick so easily; I feel fearful for him."

By watching you express yourself without putting responsibility for your feelings on others, a child learns that it is safe and acceptable to express herself fully as well. By doing so, she will know herself and generate her own path powerfully; she will have the ability to express emotions and move on. We cannot shield our children from life's challenges, but we can model a love of reality and we can provide them with freedom of self-expression, a cornerstone for emotional resilience.

Chapter Four

ℳ

Emotional Safety

Share life with a child who acts kindly and productively not because she fears you, but because she wants to of her own free will.

Children can only release stress and maintain emotional well-being when they feel completely safe to express themselves. The need to feel emotionally safe is therefore closely related to the need for freedom of self-expression. Your child will feel safe when she is treated with kindness and respect in response to her emotional expressions and when she observes you being vulnerable and seeing that other people are safe to express themselves around you.

A child learns her cues from experience: Can she make mistakes safely or will she be shamed? Can she cry with your respectful attention or will she be belittled? Can she tell you her deepest fears and find a compassionate ear? Are other people you relate to safe to express themselves and to make mistakes around you? A child who must be on guard lest she do or say the "wrong" thing does not feel safe enough to express herself for fear that her parents will judge her, belittle her, give advice, or try to change her mind. She cannot express herself authentically when she is unsure of her parents' unconditional love.

Our goal is not to raise a child who has no fears (which is impossible and unsafe), but to ensure that the natural load of anxieties finds its way out so emotional equilibrium can be maintained. A state of constant anxiety harms a child's ability to think, learn, relate, and develop. Home is the place to feel safe and to unleash emotions with the attentive listening of parents and other caregivers. A child can then let go of upsets quickly without holding on or suppressing her pain.

No matter how much we try, children will still live in a certain amount of intimidation that is natural to human beings who are small, new to the experience of being human (as far as we can tell), and dependent for survival on bigger people. As a parent, you are your child's haven and protection, the one whom she trusts and whose advocacy she relies on till she reaches full size. For her own and for your emotional well-being, make yourself a safe ally for your child. She needs to experience that you cherish her feelings, choices, and thoughts. In a counseling session, a father told me about being a safe listener to his son.

> At the park, five-year-old Herbie was sliding by himself when two other boys came by. They approached him when he was sitting at the bottom of the slide just coming off it. "Would you play with us on the carousel?" one of the boys asked Herbie.
>
> Herbie looked at them silently and didn't move. Then he went over to his father, Robert, and buried his face in Dad's coat.
>
> One of the two boys asked the father, "Why doesn't he talk?"

"I think he wants to play by himself," Robert responded.

The two boys left. The father caressed his son and said, "Do you want to keep sliding now?"

"I want to go home," Herbie answered.

"Let's go," Robert said, got up, and, hand-in-hand, they started walking away.

"Do you like to have the playground all for yourself?" Robert said, trying to guess his son's preference.

"Yes."

"And do you wish that other children wouldn't talk to you?"

"Uh-huh."

"Yes, I understand how you feel. I often prefer to do things by myself too."

"Betsy likes to play with other children," said Herbie, referring to his older sister

"Yes, I know. You are more like me. When I was a child, I often liked to play by myself and didn't want to talk to other children. It is nice to be able to do whatever you feel is right for yourself."

"Dad?"

"Yes, Herbie?"

"You know what I feel right for myself now?"

"What?"

"To go home and eat the rest of my pizza."

Herbie's father never tried to change his son's mind, to convince him of anything, or to imply that his choice was not a sound one. By respecting him so fully and sharing validating information about himself, Herbie's father created emotional safety and a heartfelt connection. With such a vote of confidence, a child can grow to trust himself and be vulnerable with his father. Your goal is to have a relationship in which your child looks forward to sharing her feelings and thoughts with you because she is confident in your unconditional vote of love.

Any doubt in a child's mind about your unequivocal support can hinder her ability to relate to you. She may respond inauthentically to avoid provoking your anger or criticism. She may refuse to tell you how she feels because the last time she tried you were too busy and didn't pay attention or were more interested in giving advice than in listening. Or, she may quickly agree to requests not because she delights in helping you or in following your instructions, but because she does not dare to assert herself. Such responses eventually rob the child of her ability to know and to trust her own feelings, and they can hinder her ability to think and to form relationships.

Many people recognize this inauthenticity years later, once they are adults. In a counseling session, a mother shared with me her childhood drive to be the best student. "I had no choice," she said. "I had to be the best and I pretended to love every minute of it. Inside, I felt helpless and afraid that if I were ever less than best, I wouldn't be loved or worthy."

Another mother told me that she often pretended to agree with her dad in order to gain his favor in competition with her sister. "My dad would suggest a solution to our fight and I would accept it, even though I was furious and needed a different outcome." Children so yearn for our acceptance that any parental act that is less than loving and respectful may arouse self-doubt. They must not only be confident that we cherish and respect them, but also that we cherish their expressions of distress when we are critical or annoyed. The ideal of raising children who experience and observe only kindness is not a common human experience. As you yearn to treat your child in the best way, be also accepting of your and her fallibility. Be honest and make it safe for your child to let you know how she feels; recognizing ways in which you may intimidate your child will help you reestablish trust whenever it seems to diminish.

As mentioned earlier, denial or judgment of children's feelings and choices is a major cause of anxiety for them. If a child feels ashamed for what she does or says, she might shut down and pretend to be the way you expect her to. Her compliant behavior can fool you so that you might be oblivious to her difficulties until bigger problems show up.

Another tool of shaming and intimidating are insults posed as "humor." Lighthearted remarks at the expense of a child build a barrier of mistrust. The hurt child is most likely to pretend to be happy with the joke while shriveling inside. I recall the story of Joseph and his grandfather.

> Six-year-old Joseph was eating his dinner with audible delight, as he was chewing with an open mouth.
>
> "Hey, Joseph, I can tell that you are eating with my eyes closed, and if I open them I can count your teeth," said Ted, Joseph's grandfather with a giggle.
>
> Joseph didn't say a word.
>
> "I am not sure how you are feeling about that remark," his father, Sam, said to Joseph in an attempt to help him feel safe. He then asked him, "Do you need to say something about it?"
>
> "Yes, how did you feel when I made that joke?" asked Grandpa Ted.
>
> Without raising his eyes Joseph responded, "Oh, it is funny."

Later, in a counseling session, Joseph said, "I just pretend that I like those jokes. I really hate them. I feel bad. He makes fun of me and calls it 'humor.'"

"Why don't you tell your grandpa how you feel?" his father asked.

"I am afraid he will get mad or fight with you, Dad," Joseph responded. "He thinks that I should enjoy his jokes."

The easiest way for a child to end an unpleasant encounter is to pretend she is happy to do whatever will please the adult. The put-down cloaked as humor is painful enough. Pretending to accept it as "a joke" saves her from further insult. Yet, when experiencing intimidation, a child is unable to experience our love. She feels confused when the person she loves most is also someone she feels unsafe to share her authentic feelings with. Over time she can conclude, "Something must be wrong with me. I can't be the way they want me to," an inner conversation that hinders self-esteem.

While creating an environment in which children feel safe, we need not be afraid of making mistakes. If we behave in fearful ways, the child absorbs our anxiety, which only adds to her self-doubt. Being overly concerned about children's sensitivities discounts their emotional ability to accept human reality, to withstand pain, to forgive, and to make their own mistakes. As long as they can express their emotions fully with parental attention, children are capable of handling difficult situations. In fact, encounters with "imperfect" parents can become growth opportunities when not constant or abusive and provided that you acknowledge your fallibility in difficult situations, validate the child's hurt feelings, and make amends.

Your Feelings and the Child's Sense of Safety

Freedom of self-expression is not identical for a child and for a parent. You have to be a caring and kind listener to your child no matter how he expresses himself, yet he cannot do the same for you, since your intense feelings can frighten him and because he takes your emotions personally. A child is not ready to take upon himself your distress. He is not the parent nor the counselor; he is not here to absorb explosions of rage or to validate a hurting parent. Therefore, express the emotions that may scare or hurt your child in the ears of another adult who is able and willing to give you attention.

You may talk to your child about feelings that don't have the potential to frighten or burden him. Make sure he is not harboring disturbing thoughts or feelings at the time; then you can tell him about your feelings, provided that your words are void of any blame or judgment of anyone. In other words, focus on yourself rather than on the fault of another. "I feel furious when my shirt is wrinkled" does not threaten anyone. In contrast, "I feel that she doesn't care about my clothes" leaves a child worried about being blamed for your feelings next time around. In addition to providing safety, avoiding blame passes on to your child the gift of being the source of his feelings, thereby being a powerful person rather than a victim.

If you grew up in a family in which you felt unsafe to air your heartfelt thoughts and desires, you may find it difficult to create one in which your child does feel secure. The reason for this is that the moment your child expresses his intense feelings, your past fear of expressing yourself may be triggered with or without your awareness of it. Naturally, you don't want to be reminded of past pain, which is why you may find yourself preventing your child from expressing himself.

Yet, we must be willing to feel uncomfortable if we are to turn the corner from denial to exuberance. We cannot afford to stop a child's expression to protect ourselves from discomfort. Instead, use S.A.L.V.E. when your child's expression sets you off: (S) Stop yourself, notice the impending reaction, let it run its course (S) silently in your mind (investigate if you have time; if not, do that later), and then put your (A) attention on the child and (L) listen. (V) Validate the child's perception and (E) empower him by refraining from easy fixing and by trusting him.

At another time you can write your reactive thoughts down and investigate their validity, relevance, who you would be without them, and how they apply to you. You can do this in writing by yourself or you may partner with an adult listener and work your way toward self-realization. By doing so, you will not need to react in ways that are scary and irrelevant to the child. Creating a safe family environment gives each one of you the opportunity to relate intimately without hurting each other, and when hurt does occur, to talk about it openly. Indeed, raising our children can propel us to raise ourselves.

Some parents say that their children are able to listen to their expression of painful emotions and show that they care. Yet, a young child who takes this role upon himself may be experiencing fear and guilt. He may be afraid that the parent cannot handle tough situations, or he might think he is the cause of the parent's upset and feel ashamed. Although we need not cover up our sadness or joy, it is scary for a child to be in the consoling role, to face a parent whose distress is constantly threatening to erupt or one who is needy and expresses weakness and inability to be a parent. To feel safe and to trust you, he needs to rely on your ability to respect his emotional limits. As he matures, a child who has been free to express himself will gradually develop the ability to listen and care about you.

Recognizing Fear-Based Behaviors

Many children, when feeling even slightly unsafe in their daily relationship, exhibit similar behaviors. Seeing any one of these fear-based behaviors lets us know that the child is not feeling emotionally safe. Some of the most common signs of fear and shame are:

- A child who feels unsafe will hide her unacceptable actions. For example, she will bother her brother when her parents are not looking. On the other hand, a child who feels safe will bother her brother without worrying about parental retaliation. In fact, she may be more likely to do so in her parents' presence, hoping for their response to her needs.

- When things go astray (a lost toy, a broken dish, or an unfair game), a child who feels shame is apt to lie because she fears her parents' reaction to what occurred. When confronted, she will stare at the floor speaking softly or saying nothing. Or she may be loud, trying to tell her "truth" convincingly. In contrast, a child who feels secure will not have a need to hide or cover up anything. Her parent will not investigate her; the child will calmly and confidently share information if needed, while keeping eye contact.

- A child who is afraid of being judged is likely to stop whatever she is doing when her parent enters the room. A child who has not developed a fear of being judged may be so absorbed that she will not notice her parent — or if she does, she will go on with her activity or invite the parent to see what she is doing.

- A fearful child will avoid asserting herself, especially if she thinks her wishes will conflict with her parents'. The self-assured child, however, will step forward and communicate, either verbally or, when young, through her actions and cues.

- Feeling unsafe hinders the child's ability to make decisions. She tries to sense what will be accepted and fears judgment. She will say, "I don't know," or use silence as a way to cause parents to choose for her and thereby secure the accepted choice.

- The fearful child may be secretive, isolated and/or develop aggressions, tics, bed-wetting, nightmares, or other symptoms of distress. The child who feels safe is communicative and relaxed with her parents.

- The ability to concentrate is severely hampered by insecurity and fear so that the child seems unable to understand things. The child who feels confident can utilize her intelligence optimally.

- A child who does not feel emotionally safe and confident will sometimes choose a careful path of pleasing. She may strive to blend in rather than be herself. She may be exceptionally well-behaved, obedient, and helpful. The self-assured child has no reason to disturb anyone nor any reason to constantly appease us or others. She will be assertive, authentic, and demonstrate her real needs as well as her playfulness and cooperation. Whether shy and private or outgoing and in charge, a child who feels free to be herself has no need to live according to anyone else's drummer.

These typical demonstrations of intimidation show up at times in most children. Even when we are completely responsive to the baby/toddler, nurse on request, sleep together as a family, and carry her on our body, there is no escape from an eventual encounter with some insecurity as she grows up. When you notice a reaction of fear in your child, even when you think you are being gentle, validate her perception: "Did you feel scared when I said, 'Stop'?" Or, when suspecting that she is concealing her feelings for fear of your disapproval, you can ask, "Would you rather not be part of the swim team? Do what you think is right for you. You know best what excites you." Over time, such encounters accompanied by your general trust of your child will eliminate her intimidation and rebuild trust between the two of you.

When a child feels safe to express herself, she will be authentic. She will maintain her emotional well-being by letting hurts out of her system through tears, verbal expressions, play, and art.

Making family relationships safe for your children creates freedom for your expression too. Home becomes a loving place that embraces you and your child's magnificence, as well as your errors and your forgiveness, in an ambiance of loving kindness.

Preventing Lying, Hiding, and Other Fear-Based Behaviors

To prevent or stop a child's habit of hiding, lying, or acting in other defensive ways, we must dissolve the fear that triggers those expressions. Freed of the fear, the child will feel comfortable to be open and honest. At times, try as you might to create such a safe environment, your child may still feel intimidated simply because he is a child. Be sensitive and respectful; avoid pushing him beyond his natural limits and don't prove that he "lied." If he hides the truth, you know he is feeling unsafe. Your goal is to alleviate the cause of his fear. In a phone session, Matthew shared with me about a time when he succeeded to provide such safety for his daughter.

> *When Matthew entered the living room, he found six-year-old Adia trying to put together a broken vase. She seemed nervous.*
>
> *"It fell by itself," Adia said without looking up.*
>
> *Matthew pondered what to say. It was a beautiful vase they had received on their wedding day from a dear friend. Feeling confused he bent down and started helping his daughter in her impossible mission.*
>
> *After a minute or so he said, "I don't think we can put it together."*
>
> *Adia stopped and burst out crying. Realizing that she was afraid to tell the truth, Matthew reassured her, "This could happen to anyone. The other day I broke a lens of a camera."*

Adia looked at her father. Feeling partially relieved she said, "I didn't know that the plant was so close to it. I pushed it aside to make room for my doll."

"Oh, I see, and then the vase fell off the shelf," Matthew said calmly and added, "Were you afraid that I would be angry at you like I was the other day?"

Adia nodded.

"I wish I wasn't angry then and I am not angry now. It was a nice vase, but I love you more. I want you to feel safe to tell me what happened."

"Dad?"

"Yes, Adia."

"Let's get the broom."

Matthew treated Adia the way most people would treat a guest who broke a valuable item by accident. Knowing that such an event leaves a person with feelings of guilt and embarrassment, we tend to do what we can to help him feel free of guilt. Matthew took full responsibility for being the cause of Adia's need to "lie." No lessons and no words can convey the value of truth better. Acts of kindness teach honesty and create the conditions that allow truth to manifest.

Naturally, you won't always be able to maintain a sense of complete safety. When you catch yourself intimidating your child, acknowledge your error and validate the child's feelings so you can re-create trust between the two of you. With time and practice, being sensitive to your child will become effortless and consistent.

The following are guiding ideas that will enhance your child's sense of safety and build trust in your relationship with him:

- Avoid evaluating your child (or others in his presence) with praise or criticism. Needing to please you and live up to expectations is a great source of anxiety for children.
- Speak kindly and respectfully to your child, both in public and in private. Preaching, scolding, interrupting, blaming, testing, or judging are unkind ways to treat anyone, child or adult, and these methods lead to fear, shame, and distrust. Express love, appreciation, and care for him with joy.
- Avoid comparing your child with anyone. Comparison is an evaluation, which creates fear and tension. When the comparison is in his favor, the child will fear the loss of your approval next time, and when the comparison favors another, he will feel hurt as well as resentful toward the other child and toward you.
- Be kind to your spouse, friends, and relatives. When observing unkind relationships, the child fears he will be treated in the same way. In addition, keep in mind that children emulate our ways.
- Encourage all the emotional expressions of children and respond with listening, validation, and kindness.
- Respect a child's safe decisions and choices. When you counter his choices, disregard his decision, or impose your choices, self-doubt and insecurity result. Instead, start by saying "Yes," so you are "forced" to find a supportive response. "Yes, you want to tear books. Here are some magazines you can tear," or "Yes, you love to play with the plastic bag on your head. Here is a paper bag. It is safe and, if you want, I can make holes for your eyes to see." Even when there is no way to support a child's action, say "yes"

to his intent, "Yes, I can see that you love to annoy your sister. Would you like to tell me about it?"

- Avoid controlling or suppressing natural childlike behaviors. Noise, giggles, messes, exuberance, and endless curiosity are natural and are needed for growth.

- Refuse to resort to punishments, time-outs, consequences, bribes, and threats. No matter what name we give these strategies, no matter how gently they are applied or how well-intended they may be, their purpose is to control children's behavior. Therefore, they induce fear and get in the way of trust between parent and child and lead to the behaviors they intend to prevent.

The Price of Controlling a Child

Although some parents claim that methods of control provide a structure that encourages youngsters to behave well and even seem content, keep in mind that seemingly peaceful, cooperative, and happy children may not actually be feeling serenity and joy, but may instead be striving to please or live up to expectations. Beneath their actions, they may be afraid to express themselves. When they comply and behave in pleasing ways, these children are only happy to please their parents, not happy to be doing what they are doing (helping, sharing, studying). This apparent "happiness" makes it hard for parents to notice the shriveling of the child's authentic way of being.

For example, a mother said to me, "When I send my daughter to her room or when I spank her, she calms down and seems to do better." The question is "Better for whom?" The child who complies out of fear is not doing better but worse. She has given up on her own direction in favor of keeping herself safe and satisfying her parents.

No matter how gently or "cooperatively" one establishes punishments, time-outs, or consequences, each method incurs a cost—one we are often unaware of until, sometimes years later, the child demonstrates a lack of authenticity or assertiveness, depression, addictions, violence, or self-destructive behavior. A child cannot experience the parent's love while being controlled by him/her. Instead, she becomes dependent yet isolated and will later need to control others in passive or active ways.

Assertiveness (sometimes interpreted as "defiance") is a demonstration of will and therefore of emotional strength. The giving up of the will by the obedient child is a demonstration of fear and of an emotional handicap. As the Russian educator L.S. Vygotsky writes, "People with great passions, people who accomplish great deeds, people who possess strong feelings, people with great minds and a strong personality rarely come out of good little boys and girls."

Gentle ways of controlling fool both the parent and the child. A child who cooperates with consequences, a time-out, or any variation of such measures with ease or even smiles is too insecure to voice her hurt and often out of touch with her own feelings. She must believe that her parents are doing the right thing and so she concludes that her sense of wrongness is a mistake not to be trusted.

Even what some parents call "natural" consequences is mostly parent-imposed and therefore causes the same harm and mistrust as punishment. If it is natural, it occurs on its own. For example, a father told me that the "natural" consequence of his son not finishing his chores is that he will not go to his friend's house, as he now must stay home and do his chores. However, if a child was expected to wash dishes and didn't, the only natural consequence is that the dishes are dirty. Canceling his play date is a punishment imposed by the parent against the child's will. The child will fear such punishment like any other. To test the validity of this observation ask yourself how you would feel if your spouse told you that since you didn't mow the lawn like you planned, you now must do it and skip your yoga class.

You may choose to skip yoga, and the child who neglected the dishes may choose, after you express your feelings, to wash the dishes before going over to his friend's; however, such choices must come from respectful communication of the people involved and based on their authentic preferences. You can kindly offer to wash the dishes or find some other considerate solution. You can also find out why the chore wasn't done, and you may discover some need for change in the work loads or expectations. It is the controlling aspect that creates disconnection and fear, not the actual decision and solution. When you offer to help, the child learns to offer help unconditionally. The fear that he will take advantage of you, as mentioned in the chapter on love, hampers your freedom to be generous and passes that fear on to your child.

When controlled, human beings feel humiliated and isolated. When gentle coercive ways are applied, the child is only confused and may think that her sense of humiliation is inadequate and should be suppressed. "My parents are so nice; how come I feel so bad? Something must be wrong with me." In response, the parent is fooled by the child's compliance and believes that the control is benefiting the child while she is actually feeling hurt and confused.

In our most desperate moments, we need to recall that fear-inducing disciplinary measures lead to fear-based compliance, not to thriving children. Since what we are striving for can be achieved with dignity, there is no need to fall back on old methods that hurt the child, violate his autonomy, and damage your relationship with him. When your child feels safe to be himself, he will act with competence, not in order to please you but because he wants to succeed. He will be considerate and kind not because he fears you but because he loves you.

Making It Safe to Express Unavoidable Fear

There are causes of fears over which we have no control, yet we can empower a child to free himself from their grip. Causes can range from birth, medical procedures, or separation from mother, to a scary experience at the playground, a story, a movie, a visitor whose voice is loud or who looks scary to the child, as well as other unknown causes. If the home is not safe for self-expression or the child's feelings are denied, those scary experiences gradually build up and create emotional disturbances. All emotional difficulties are simply stories the mind makes up based on painful experiences. Fear is a major component in a child's creation of limiting conclusions about herself, and about life. The fear does not always manifest in a straightforward way but may show up as other fears and anxieties. It may be fear of the dark, of falling asleep, of animals, of certain people, of touch, of being away from home, and more. Some of these fears are a natural passage of growth; they easily pass when the child can safely vent them.

As discussed earlier, the tendency to "calm" down the child gets in the way of his ability to liberate himself from those anxieties. By trying to stop his expression, we demonstrate our own discomfort with his fear, leaving the child even more afraid to feel how scared he is. He may also doubt himself and think, "Something is wrong with me. I shouldn't be afraid." The fear of fear itself can be more painful and limiting than whatever is scary at the moment. Therefore, any time you notice fear in your child, validate it without dramatizing, so he can be at peace with his fear.

Your calm in the face of his panic will help your child accept that these experiences are a part of being human and not something to avoid or to turn into a trauma story in the mind. If he is scared of the dark you can validate and then listen to him, "I know how you feel. In the dark we can't see what is around us and we can imagine scary things." If he clings to you when a dog comes by, lift him up into your secure arms. Be on your child's side and validate with "The dog is so big. Are you feeling scared? I am glad that I can hold you secure in my arms." It is better not to say, "He is a nice dog. You can caress him," etc., because it denies the child's perception. Letting the child know that he is simply experiencing a normal human emotion will enable him to keep telling you about his fears without feeling bad about himself. If, through childhood, the flow of talking about fears is unhindered, their grip will naturally ease over time.

Even severely bad experiences don't leave scars when spoken about or expressed through words, tears, art, play therapy, and other emotional expressions. Adults who were not able to talk about their painful or scary childhood experiences tend to suffer. However, in their counseling sessions these adults discover that the most painful part was not what happened to them, but the loneliness, disconnection and the fear of talking about it.

Humans can handle a huge range of painful experiences if they can talk about them or, when very young, they can express themselves and have their thoughts and feelings acknowledged and validated. In my counseling work, again and again I encounter adults who were molested and abused and do not suffer ill effects, while others with similar experiences are deeply in pain that cripples their daily living. The difference is mostly in the child's ability to talk to someone who listened, validated his feelings, and let him know that he could handle it. Those who carry emotional scars find quick healing when they explore the many painful thoughts they have been living with in isolation. Not that these experiences were not painful, but the inability to recover came from the isolation and fear of talking about what happened.

Most of the time your child's scary experiences are going to be benign, and only the fear of talking about them can inflate them into stories of damaging impact. When a child shares his deepest emotions and thoughts, he can heal from painful and scary experiences, and his mind won't turn benign events into traumatic stories.

Safe to Express Hate

In most of us the word "hate" evokes discomfort and fear of hurting one's sense of worthiness. When a child screams that she despises her sister or hates us, we may feel a desire to dam up the torrent of "unwanted" emotions. Yet hate is not about facts or truth, nor is it an action that we need to fear. Like anger, hate covers up other emotions that must be revealed and expressed so the child can see what is true for her. Even when the cause of the feeling is based on misunderstanding, the feeling is still experienced; only after the child expresses herself fully is she able to converse and reexamine the facts and possibilities.

If we want to get away from hateful verbal expressions, we must help a child get in touch with the emotions that trigger the hate. Our task is to make it safe for children to express the emotions that lead to hate, while providing verbal tools and settings that prevent hurting one another. When the child unleashes feelings, he can notice that reality is much kinder than the drama he made up. In one of my workshops, a parent told a story in which validation of underlying emotions dissipated hate:

> *Eight-year-old Gabe wanted the whole cake for himself. When Grandma divided it between himself and his cousin, he said to her, "I hate you. You never let me have what I want."*
>
> *"Are you disappointed because you will only get half of the cake and you wanted more?" she asked.*
>
> *"Yes," Gabe said, "I want the whole cake. You bought it for me. It is my visit. Laura wasn't supposed to be here anyway."*
>
> *"Oh, I see, you wish to be the only one who gets the cake."*

> *"Yes. Me and me," responded Gabe with a spark in his eyes.*
> *"I know how that feels when – " Grandma started, but Gabe interrupted, "Grandma, can I have strawberries with my cake?"*

Children often move on faster than we realize when their expressions are not denied and they feel safe to be authentic. Gabe's Grandma was not fond of the word "hate." Yet, she did not want to take away Gabe's sense of trust and security expressed by his candid expression. Instead of focusing on the word, her question helped Gabe see the underlying feeling of disappointment and his wish to have the whole cake. She never negated his words. He could then let go of his feelings and embrace the joy of the moment the way it is. Over the years and after more repetitions of this kind, Gabe may express himself with "I feel disappointed" or "I feel angry; I wish I could have the whole cake" instead of "I hate you." As he matures further, he will also be able to let go of expectations before they give rise to any painful feelings at all and stay joyful in the face of deviation from his plans.

Hate Between Children

Ideally, the distress of feeling hateful toward another child is best absorbed by the parents or other loving adults. By making it safe for a child to vent her feelings in our ears, we can minimize her need to do so in the ears of a sibling or friend who might take it seriously and feel hurt. You can let your child know that when she feels angry with another child, she can come and tell you all about it and can count on you to listen empathically and without judging.

Children often resolve their conflicts on their own and express hate to each other in spite of our best efforts. They are ingenious at creating scenes that may seem painful to adults and yet are a valuable psychodrama for them. Often they exchange demeaning remarks in a way that leaves all of them evenly in power. But when power is uneven, children, being self-centered by nature, are likely to take such comments personally and to feel hurt or insecure. At such times we might make the error of rushing to undo the hate by negating it with something like "Oh, no, we love her; she is smart and wonderful," and give her a hug. The child, however, is affected by our anxiety more than by our words. She learns that the insult must have been terrible and that she should feel bad. Next time she might feel even worse. What we can do instead is empower a child in the face of insults by asking her how she feels and by validating her expressed emotion so she can re-create her sense of worth by looking at what she knows to be true. For instance:

> Roy came over and complained to his aunt, "Maryann called me 'stupid' and told me that she hates my guts."
>
> "How are you feeling when you believe her?" his aunt asked.
>
> "Stupid," he said.
>
> "So, do you think that you are really stupid or bad?" she inquired.
>
> "No," Roy answered confidently, "I know that I am smart and very nice." After a moment of thought he left and returned to his play.

Empowering a child to stay in touch with her own value in the face of offending words will better prepare her for future human encounters. Roy's aunt helped Roy notice that he feels stupid only when he takes his friend's words for truth; his own thought about himself fills him with confidence. In other words, she asked him questions that helped him see how it is up to him which thought he takes seriously. If you want to ask such effective questions, look for the general question—"Which thought is painful to you?"—and translate it to the event the child is describing. Our communication may result in a realization like Roy's, or it may bring tears and the release of pent-up anxiety or self-doubt. Whichever it is, it will propel the child toward recognition of her inner knowing and strength.

If hateful feelings are not spoken in the ears of an empathic parent, they will be heard again and again in the ears of children. We can minimize the amount of resentment between children by meeting their individual needs and by listening to them when they feel rage and hate. The more accepting we are of the child's feelings, the more she will come to us and spare her siblings and friends. When we listen and validate, the child is likely to get in touch with her other feelings, those that are masked by pointing fingers at her sibling or friend. (See pages 143 - 149 in Chapter Three, "Listening to Children's Anger.") In time, she will learn to feel those personal emotions and skip the reaction of blame and hate.

"I Wish I Could Get Rid of My Sister"

There are situations when the idea of validating may seem absurd; yet, even then it is what heals and connects. For example, a child may express a wish such as "I wish my sister was dead. I could just kill her for this." We may get caught up in the passion and worry that the threat might be real or that the child shouldn't use such violent words. Feeling fearful, we are likely to negate the child's feelings. Yet negating, criticizing, or punishing a child who expresses such intense emotions and violent fantasies will cause him to bury his pain and feel desperate in his isolation, making aggressive behavior more likely to erupt. Indeed, feeling lonely and unsafe to express emotions is one of the causes of violence. Listening to such distress will be easier when you remember that it is only an emotion that he is expressing.

Validating violent feelings does not mean you endorse the fantasies expressed as something to act on. Indeed, if you support your child's expression of hateful emotions, you make violent action less plausible and kindness more probable. Just like the S of S.A.L.V.E. for you, your child also needs to let the painful Self-Talk out of his system; but unlike you, he cannot do it silently on his own. Provide the listening so that he can unleash the drama. You might say, "I understand. You are so upset with Katie that you wish you could get rid of her. I know how it is to be so upset with someone." You can even provide insight into the commonality of such feelings and fantasies by sharing your own experience: "I remember wishing my brother would fall off the cliff." If you offer such a memory, do not

dwell on it (unless the child asks for it). It is your child's spot-
light, not yours; your memory is only a way to include and
validate your child's feelings.

When you allow your child to feel and express violent emotions, and when you confirm that everyone experiences violent
emotions at times, he can release the pain and is likely to get in
touch with the feelings that prompt his rage without adding
the burden of guilt and shame.

Hate, like anger, is a function of the mind manufacturing a
blame story; someone "did it" to him. Ask validating questions
that help him recognize and own his feelings and let go of his
victim story by sorting out the thoughts that rob him of his
power. Blaming is always about the past, which leaves the child
helpless because there is nothing he can do about it. He has no
power over his sister and over what she did, but he can have
power over his own feelings and actions in the present. The
child learns to distinguish the blame drama from his own powerful self.

A child can become frightened and guilty about his own
violent fantasies. He needs to know that these fantasies are normal and don't affect your love for him. Sometimes a child needs
to express himself for a while and in variety of ways; a toddler
can play it out on a doll, an older child can act or draw, and a
teenager may want to talk a lot and to write, run, or make
music. By accepting the expression of intense feelings without
acting on them, we grow to live with intimacy, vulnerability,
and the ability to love and to be responsible for our own emotions and choices.

Talking about a wish for one's brother or sister to vanish gives voice to the intensity of the child's feelings and does not usually indicate an intention to hurt. Actual violence occurs when children are oppressed and after years of not being able to be themselves, they become resigned and unable to feel connected. They may appear peaceful on the outside and even successful at school; yet by living a life scripted by their elders, they feel depressed, emotionally isolated, and convinced that no one can hear them nor cares to. This isolation and pain renders them helpless to the point of despair.

Normal forms of sibling rivalry are not expressions of such despair and the children do not intend to cause real harm. If you are not sure whether your child's hateful or violent expressions are within a healthy range, you should seek help. Most aggressive youth I have encountered in my work experience, respond extremely well to counseling that gives them back their dignity and their emotional strength.

For the child whose life flows unhindered, hate is just another feeling he expresses, and then he moves on. It is *unexpressed* hate that drives a child to agression, name-calling or disturbing, while sufficient venting of intense feelings prevents those outcomes. The following account of an adolescent in the grip of hate illustrates the power of expressing his feelings to rebuild the bridge of love:

> *Eleven-year-old Jay started his therapy session by expressing intense hatred for his nine-year-old sister. He talked about his violent fantasies and vowed never to have anything to do with her. In fact, he wanted to leave home because there was no way he could live in*

the same house with her. He spent more than half an hour cursing and yelling, drawing fantasy scenes of her death, wishing he was an only child, and finally crying. He expressed his dismay at the fact that his parents "ruined his life" by having his sister. He thought that if they loved him, they should now get rid of her.

Then Jay began to talk about his sister's intolerable qualities, like always needing to be first, declaring she can do anything better, and getting extremely upset when she is losing in a game.

After the stream of talking ceased, I asked Jay to focus on his own feelings. "How do you feel and behave when you have all these judgments about your sister and nothing changes?"

"Angry, hateful, resentful," he said.

"What do you want for yourself?" I asked.

"Nothing," he said, "or, maybe time away from my sister. I feel resentful when she is around me, getting attention, acting like a princess."

"What would you be like without that thought?" I asked.

Jay gazed at me with disbelief. "Without the thought about my sister? Oh boy, that would be great," he said. "I would be free and happy and my sister's way of being would not matter to me."

"So you would enjoy that?"

"Oh yes." He started laughing, "I think I make a big drama out of my sister."

"Would you like to be free of the thought of you resenting your sister?"

"No. I want to hate her," he said. Then, surprised by his own words he said, "Gee, this is weird. Why would I want such pain?"

"It must have some reward for you."

Jay was silent.

"What is the reward for resenting and blaming your sister?" I asked.

"I get to see myself as the better one," he said, "and maybe I get to control my parents."

At this point Jay could experience himself as the author of his perceptions and his feelings. He began to empathize with his sister and, deeply saddened, described what he thought she was facing. "She must feel like a loser with me as her older brother, so she keeps trying to get ahead," he said. His care for his sister became as strong as his initial rage. Then, free to focus on his own aspirations, Jay spent the rest of his session making new plans for himself.

There are no final and permanent solutions; we must accept the cycles of relationships and attend to them as they come and go. For the moment, Jay was able to empathize and see his sister's point of view. As life went on, he kept getting annoyed with her, expressing himself, becoming connected and happy, and then getting annoyed and hateful again. When, through each cycle of bad feelings, a child expresses himself fully in our ears, he is empowered to make choices rather than react from the old movies. He can be in charge of his perceptions rather than make up a victim's story to live by. In the process, he provides us with information about both children's needs so that we are better able to care for them.

It is easy to get caught up in expecting outcomes. However, we cannot assume that any time our children feel safe enough to express their venom, it will dissipate. If we get caught up in expecting results, we miss the opportunity to listen and to connect with the child. For example, sometimes a child will refuse to play with a sibling or a friend even after expressing his feelings.

Parents may then rush to generate a "result" and say, "Okay, now you got your feelings out, forgive and play together." This is what happened when Sylvia refused to join the Monopoly® game with her cousin.

> Eight-year-old Sylvia was upset with her cousin, Timmy, because he took her bike without permission. When Sylvia wanted to ride, she found her bike gone. Her mother listened and validated her feelings and as soon as Timmy returned from his ride, her dad put her bike away to ensure that no one would take it again without Sylvia's agreement. Timmy apologized for disappearing with her bike without her knowledge and promised not to do it again.
>
> When Timmy invited Sylvia to play Monopoly® a short while later, she refused and stuck her tongue out to him. "It is time to make peace now," her dad said. "We listened to you, and he apologized. Come on, go play." But, the more her parents expected a peaceful resolution, the more Sylvia dug in her feet. She was not ready to move on. Finally her parents shrugged their shoulders and got out of the way. Sylvia went into her room feeling satisfied that she prevented her cousin from playing Monopoly®. Five minutes later she came out and invited him to her indoor hammock.

Children tend to be much faster than adults in letting go of resentment; but like adults, they must be the authors of their choices. Expecting that your child will be free of the mind's need to be right is more than most of us can model. Therefore, your goal is not to fix the dispute or erase the feelings, but to listen and enable your child to make his own choices authentically and with dignity.

While feeling hateful, the child's greatest fear is that he is a bad person and that if you knew what he was thinking and fantasizing, you wouldn't love him. Therefore, when he feels safe to express his hateful feelings fully and still be cherished by you, the goal has been achieved. Knowing that your love doesn't waver because of his hateful thoughts, he will be able to express himself fully every time he needs to, and you will be able to rest assured, knowing that the channels of communication between the two of you are open. With time, he will be able to move away from hate altogether by recognizing that he is the source of whatever thoughts ignite his emotions. Maybe he will even learn to distinguish his mind's voice from who he really is and gain true peace and freedom.

Feeling Hate Toward Parents

Hateful words may be directed not only at siblings, but also at parents. As human beings we are bound to make mistakes that violate our children's dignity. When we do so — interrupt, impose, control, or demean — and the child vents her hate toward us, we can listen, validate, and then acknowledge our errors and regrets so she can feel safe to be open with us. Even when the child's hate is the result of your safety measures, her dignity is still violated. Validating her feelings and acknowledging the way we have done things (even when unavoidable), will dissipate the bad feelings.

A young child who is not yet conversational will feel validated when her hate is acknowledged with your description of the facts: "Mommy didn't buy the candy that you wanted. Yucky

Mommy"; "Gee, did I scare you with my yells?"; or "You didn't like that woman who peeked into the sling?"

She will feel reassured to know that you are aware of her feelings and that you love her just the same. As a child's verbal ability matures, such discord can spur dialogues that enrich and deepen your understanding of her personality.

When a child's hate is directed at us, validating her feelings can be complicated by our personal reaction. Yet when we care for our own emotions in a supportive, separate setting or by investigating our own thoughts, we can then give love where it is most needed. Here is an example of S.A.L.V.E. in action while a parent is "under fire" from a child.

> Five-year-old Lea kept saying, "I hate you, Mom," and Betty, her mother, felt sad and worried. Initially, Betty's defensive emotions got in the way and she tried to stop Lea's expression. When Lea's expression persisted, Betty took care of herself in a counseling session, after which she felt able to empathize with her daughter.
>
> The next time Lea said, "I hate you," Betty responded, "Gee, that can be painful. I am glad you are telling me because I want to know how you feel." Then she asked, "Will you tell me about your hate toward me?"
>
> Lea looked at her mom fiercely and said, "You didn't make the right breakfast and you yelled when I was slow."
>
> "So you wanted to have pancakes and not eggs?"
>
> "Yes."
>
> "And did you want to keep dressing your doll when I rushed you to get ready to go?"
>
> "Just don't yell, Mom. It hurts."

"I can understand how you feel. I am glad you told me. I, too, like to stay gentle even when I am in a rush. Do you think I can always do that?"

Lea thought for a moment and then said, "No, you can't, Mom. That's all right, Mom. But the pancakes..."

"Yes, you would like to choose what you eat; I can do that much of the time."

Lea nodded, looking satisfied.

Then Betty added, "It must have felt painful to hate me."

"No, Mom. It just felt hateful."

Becoming aware of Lea's feeling, Betty has gradually found ways to eliminate many of these frustrating moments, but not all. She made sure to validate Lea's possible hateful feelings when needed. After two days, Lea said, "Mom, I love you and me. When I say that I hate you, I don't really; I just want to make you do what I want." She smiled and so did Mom.

"Do you know that I love you?" asked Betty.

"Yes, even when I hate you, Mom, which I don't really," and she wrapped her arms around her mother in an embrace.

Lea had accumulated hateful thoughts for a while before she received her mother's validation. However, if occasional feelings of hate are acknowledged as they come, children can let go of those very fast. In addition, hateful words often don't have the same heavy meaning as they do for adults:

Terry asked Mom to read him a book. "I am going to pick up the checkers game off the floor and then I will read to you," said Mom.

"Oh no, Mom," Terry whined. "Read to me now."

"I know you like me to read to you right away. I will be quick," said Mom.

> Terry stamped his feet and said, "I hate you."
> "Yes, I know," said his mom while finishing col-
> lecting the game.
> After reading, Dad invited the family to eat lunch.
> "I want Mom to make my sandwich," declared Terry.
> "I thought you hated her," said Dad.
> "That was then," responded Terry as a matter
> of fact.

When your child shows signs of resentfulness toward you, encourage her to express it to you directly. Remember that hate is an external expression of other emotions and recognize that your child's feelings of hatred are about her, even when their content relates to you. You can learn about yourself from what she says, but her expression is not about you. If you get defensive about what she is saying, gently shift your attention back to your child. Instead of insisting that she love you, reassure her of your love by listening and seeing her point of view. She will then understand that hating does not change the love she feels toward you or your love toward her. In the intimate connection that you and your child will have, she may even be able to get a glimpse at distinguishing who she really is from her mind's dramas.

Being Helpful, Not Scary

Sometimes an emotionally charged reaction from us may scare a child. This occurs when the child acts unsafely or when we take his actions or words personally. Keep in mind that a child's actions are not directed at you. He is not out there to bug you and make your life difficult, but simply to take care of

himself. When hurting someone or something, a child is expressing a need and a feeling; if acting unsafe, he is innocent in his
pursuit, regardless of how many times you told him. (How
many times do adults have to be told certain things before those
become second nature?)

Nothing your child says or does deserves your anger, judgment, or deprivation of your love. Even while stopping him
from hurting someone or himself, your actions and words can
connect the two of you with love and care. When you stop him
with an expression of care, the child will perceive you as being
on his side and he will not develop fear of you. For example,
yelling "Stop grabbing her doll right now" will keep your child
feeling scared and worthless. If instead you use validating statements like "You wish to play with the doll and Ruth is playing
with it," and you offer your attention and/or a solution, the
child will perceive you as caring and himself as worthy.

When you scare your child, he does not perceive you as
being on his side, but as being someone who is out to get him,
somewhat like the police. Therefore he will fear you and tend
to go against you. Even when you have taken a swift action to
save him from harm, validate the fear he may have felt and find
a way to meet the need that prompted his unsafe action. Whenever you scare your child, communicate your feelings and offer
a solution rather than a lesson.

> *Upon entering the playroom, Dana choked a scream
> when she saw her son Sean sitting on the windowsill.
> They were living on the fourth floor, and although the
> window was closed, she was afraid that he would
> develop a habit of sitting there also when it was open.*

> *Dana controlled herself; she fetched a stool and put it by the window.*
> *"You like looking at the street," she said "Here. You can stand on the stool and see it safely." She helped him down and kissed him. Then she added, "Sean, when I saw you sitting on the window, I felt very scared."*
> *He looked at her and said, "But, Mom, I won't fall."*
> *"I know, but I still feel scared. I will leave this stool here for you. Will you promise me to use it when you wish to look down at the street and to avoid sitting on the window?"*
> *"Yes, I can see just fine from here."*
> *"Thank you, Sean," said a calm Dana.*

Dana had already told her son not to sit on the windowsill. She could have easily gone back to the old, useless, "How many times do I have to tell you...?" Instead she offered a solution while sharing her feelings in a way that did not blame the child. She did not say, "You scared me," but "I feel scared." She even validated his sense of being safe, yet made the request in honor of her own need. When connected to our feelings and when not blamed or scolded, a child can easily respond to our requests. If your child trusts you and knows you are always on his side, he will respond to you as one does when facing his ally, and with time, your child will learn to treat others in the same way.

Chapter Five

❦

Autonomy and Power

What children need are cooperative parents

Children often feel helpless because they are small and inexperienced in a complex, big, and fast world — so many machines they can't touch, big people and animals the may fear, places they can't go to on their own, heights they cannot reach, things they need help with, events they find scary, and speeds they cannot grasp. Many of their upsets result from feeling helpless.

Children need to feel that they have the power to generate responses to their needs. Unlike adults, children are not ready to give up on what they want in the present for the sake of the future. They need to know that the people around them take their immediate choices seriously. As with other emotional deprivations, a child struggling with a sense of helplessness, or deprived of feeling that she is in control of her life, may become angry, aggressive, or depressed.

Although you cannot eliminate your child's sense of helplessness, you can dramatically improve her chances of experiencing herself as autonomous and powerful. The young child or baby can affect her environment through you, and she needs you to keep being her "power extension" into whatever is beyond her reach. Sometimes that entails doing things for her, but more often it means getting out of the way and making her path safe and nurturing. By making the physical and social environments safe and healthy, you can eliminate the need to restrict or direct her. She can then choose and direct her own activities, foods, timetable, and interests within the safe environment you have created.

Children often feel helpless and at the mercy of the adults who care for them, in spite of their parents' loving intentions. Interrupted by ringing telephones while playing with a parent, they suffer the ignominy of being put on hold while their parent speaks to the offending party. They sometimes endure the insults of being told what to do, when to be quiet, and how to accommodate the adult's needs when their own needs are not consistently respected. For example, children are often criticized for interrupting adults; yet many adults interrupt children and talk "over their heads" as a matter of course. Being at the mercy of every passing event or arbitrary decision is a reality for much of a child's life in this culture.

There are ways we render a child helpless without even thinking about it. We often design life without giving the child a vote, even though our choices affect her life. Including children in our lives, as is done in a tribe, is unlikely to interest them unless we farm, build, or engage in other participatory types of physical activities. Watching Mom as she writes, reads, or does her banking lacks a motion to observe or an opportunity to partake. What occurs is not indicative of what is going on; the content of the book may be exciting, but the toddler only sees Dad sitting and glancing at a book.

One common example is taking a child on errands. The child wishes to continue with whatever she is doing; yet she is interrupted, strapped in a car seat, and carried around for no goal of her own. She is expected to be the "mature" one, accompanying the adult on her path. We would not enjoy such an experience ourselves, and we would not ask a friend to follow us on our errands. A young child has no idea that our errands benefit her; an older one may understand that, but still be disinterested in partaking. For a child, most errands are boring and motionless, made up of periods of waiting and then sitting in the car.

Although a young child may enjoy grocery shopping, as she gets older it becomes fun only if she gets a toy or a candy, which can be the cause of more frustrations. In this area, too, human experience has changed from picking up food in the field or even in an old-fashioned little food store to shopping in the over-stimulating and seductive supermarket of today, which often leaves a young child frustrated. Some parents are skillful at engaging a child in shopping and the outing is then enjoyable; but for most parents, doing errands with children is often a struggle.

To prevent this particular scenario or minimize it, do most of your errands and appointments when your spouse or another person can care for your child. When the child is young and physically in need of the mother, the father can do most of the family errands and shopping; single parents may need to find friends and family for support. In this way, the mother or father need not drag the youngster away from her interests.

Another solution is to make the outing oriented toward the child's interests: plan to go to the park, the beach, or to Grandma's house and do only one short errand on the way. Many stressed youngsters calm down simply by cutting the outings down to bare necessities.

Parents sometimes wonder why children can't grow up, as in the old days, observing adults' lives and integrating themselves as they feel ready. This can happen when the adults share a natural and active life. When the community works together, such as laboring in the field, building, cooking, and making crafts, a child can follow with interest or play around doing her own things. Our modern lives often don't provide such community nor such safety and freedom. We may miss it, but crying over the changes that have occurred is not a useful way to celebrate the present. Life is a constant change, and we must adopt and invent new ways of growing up all the time.

Including the child in what we do, as in washing the dishes, gardening, and cooking, is still with us. However, when what we do has no physical action, and when our activities prevent the child from doing what she needs, she will feel helpless and frustrated. One human being's need cannot be met by drowning the needs of another, at least not without a price. In addition, most of what we do in our home and yard is not what the child will focus on as she grows up. She needs to engage in intellectual and other skill-building activities in which she is interested and that will support her development.

Another route to helplessness is the tendency of some parents to expect a child to accomplish certain things, behave, learn, be interested, or socialize based on "norms" rather than on the child's inclination. For example, parents often call me in distress about their child's behavior while with a group of peers or due to problems in public settings like restaurants. When I suggest that they avoid taking a child to a playgroup or a class when she is not able to handle it, parents share their concern about the child's social needs. However, the child who spends her afternoon struggling with other toddlers or children is not having her social needs met. Instead of having a good time with friends, she experiences failing to relate and failing to please her parent, and feeling helpless about both. Would you go back to a social group in which you were not getting along with others? Like an adult, a child who is not successful in a social setting needs a different one or maybe just time to socialize with her parent.

Many children cannot sit quietly in a restaurant. If your child has a chance to exert her energy for a while, she may be able to sit for the duration. If not, a restaurant is not a place that respects her needs. When we impose our desires on a child just because we have the power to do so, she can feel helpless and, with time, also resentful. Instead of listening to the media or to Grandma, observe and listen to your child, regardless of all the opinions. She is growing up here and now while none of the well-meaning advice-givers are. She is the expert on her own needs.

The tendency to have expectations can render a child helpless, even when those aspirations are not outwardly expressed. For example, we may imply, even very subtly, that sharing is desirable, that the toddler would start using the toilet, that a child should be quiet, empathic, grateful, or polite. The child can feel helpless and inadequate when she is unable to fulfill our aspirations, or when able but not inclined to do so of her own volition. She may express a desire to stay a baby to escape the burden of expectations; she may become grumpy or she may do what we wish just to get the approval or get us off her back, all the while feeling powerless.

Another way we take power away from children is to deny their personal choices. If you select an instrument your child should study, a sport she should play, her outings and activities, the time she should eat, or the clothes she must wear, you inadvertently rob her of the experience of affecting her own life. With such experiences her inner sense of helplessness may eventually lead to rebellion and aggression or to unhealthy compliance and depression.

As you release your personal agendas for your child and grant her the power to generate her own life, you may need to protect her freedom. We baby-proof the house to prevent physical hurts and allow the youngster freedom inside a safe home. Likewise, we can childproof the greater environment, including the type of media, foods, and toys she is exposed to and the social circle she is in contact with while she is young.

A child's freedom is dependent on our ability to make her life safe without having to control her. Spending the day in a natural setting prevents having to restrict a child's play, as you would have to do in a city street. Socializing with people she enjoys and feels capable around, she can play independently and without needing your intervention.

The degree to which you protect the environment is a matter of your lifestyle and parenting choices. Every parent controls the environment to some degree. Most parents protect their children from exposure to weapons, drugs, some of the news or media that exposes brutality, and perhaps cigarettes, alcohol, coffee, etc. You don't display these items in your home and then control your child by forbidding her to touch them. Instead you just don't expose her to them.

The child's sense of autonomy and power is not a function of being able to access everything that is available in our society, but rather of a day-to-day freedom in her home and social environment. For instance, if you take your child to a candy store and then forbid her from eating candy, she will feel resentful and helpless. If you do not go to the candy store and you provide healthy treats at home, she will feel autonomous and content. You provide leadership in terms of the direction of the family life so that your child has freedom to trust herself. As she grows older she will be exposed to more and more of what is available; feeling secure in herself, she will make choices based not on social pressures but on her authentic preferences and values.

If your relationship with your child is one of trust rather than control, she will take your wisdom and guidance seriously, because she knows you are on her side. This trust will be handy when she becomes engaged with the community and society at large. Instead of resenting your ideas because of seeing you as the one controlling and negating her, she will seek your advice as her loving ally.

As we saw in the previous chapter, some parents voice a concern that the child who is not controlled will take advantage of them. Keep in mind that when a child is not living in fear that her power will be taken away (that she will be controlled, coerced, or directed), she has no need to "take advantage" of anyone. Her desire is only to take care of herself, and when respected, she thrives. A thriving child is too busy and happy to bother with negative strategies.

Dissolving a Child's Aggression

Children often resort to aggression when overloaded with a sense of helplessness. No matter how much we try, being a human involves feeling helpless. When in balance and if fully expressed, feeling helpless is a natural and useful part of our existence. When out of balance and when not fully acknowledged and expressed, recurring helplessness can cause anger, aggression, and, on the other side, resignation and depression. Therefore, we need not only prevent taking away the child's power, but we also want to provide ways for him to express helplessness and to experience power in safe ways.

The most common overt way a child expresses helplessness is by negating and violating others. However, when parents are supportive of his unique expressions, a child finds playful and creative ways to regenerate his sense of power. A father asked my advice about his three-year-old who was throwing paper all over the kitchen floor. After the session, his inclination to stop his son's action changed:

> Since the family had moved to another area of the city, three-year-old Chris was displaying signs of stress. He was grumpy and constantly whining and crying over every little thing. One day he came into the kitchen and started emptying the paper and cans out of the recycling bins and throwing them all over the kitchen.

Seeing the recycling strewn about, his father responded with a dramatic "Oh no!" which seemed to give Chris the sense of power he was looking for: "Aha, I got him."

Father picked up all the paper and cans and put them back in the bins so that Chris could repeat his self-made "therapy" again and again. Each time Chris threw the stuff out, his father responded with a louder and more dramatic "Oh no," followed by a playful, "I am putting it back," and then pleading, "Oh, please don't throw it again." The game ended with the recycling all over the kitchen floor and Dad "giving up" in exhaustion.

For a couple months Chris continued to initiate this game and each time his father gasped dramatically and then picked up the recycling and put all the stuff back into the bins to be thrown out all over again with great laughter. All the while, father trusted his son's need to play this game to gain a sense of power and autonomy. One day Chris stopped dumping the recycling on the floor and never did it again. His irritability and disturbing behaviors diminished and he seemed excited about his new home.

Many parents intuitively empower children in similar ways simply because they respect them and wish to participate in their play. For example, when the child dashes off as Dad is trying to snap up his pajamas, Dad plays along, going after the child in hot pursuit. Although this game may seem long and tiring to the parent, eventually the child has enough, for he is satisfied in his need to feel powerful.

It is crucial not to take away a child's power. If you are the one to stop the game or to control its direction, you are in power and the child feels helpless all over again. Doing this cancels most of the emotional benefits of the game for the child, and such interruption leads to struggle, making it take even longer to heal the anger that ensues than it would take to let the game continue until the child decides to finish it. On the other hand, a long and enjoyable power game leaves everyone happy and feeling connected.

Although for Chris there were observable results, often parents cannot put their finger on any specific outcome. It is crucial not to develop expectations for quick behavioral changes. Most emotional benefits don't have an immediate visible manifestation, but show up gradually or unexpectedly. Often parents realize months later that some difficult behavior is no longer present in the child. In addition, we can never know what was prevented. Parents can notice a general contentment and other improvements. We have to trust the child for initiating these games and for deriving benefit from them. While knowing that they are playing a game, children get the benefit from the drama as if it were real. The following example illustrates yet another child's playful approach to achieving a sense of power.

> *One evening Kirk hung his shirt on the doorknob and went to the bathroom to get ready for bed. When he came back his shirt was gone. Melanie, his three-year-old daughter, was standing by the door with a gleeful smile on her face. "Oh no, where's my shirt?" said Kirk, acting surprised as Melanie giggled merrily.*
>
> *Thus began a bedtime ritual. Every night Kirk made sure to hang his shirt on the same knob and to let Melanie know "My shirt is on the door knob, don't hide it...," and Melanie responded to the invitation, hid Dad's shirt, and excitedly waited for him to discover his loss. This went on until, a few months later,*

Melanie had had enough, as her need to replenish her
sense of power was satisfied for the time being.

You need not be concerned that your child will construe such play as license to disturb or mess things up. On the contrary, children are very clear about the distinction between play and reality. Supporting their need to play these games allows them a safe outlet for their pent-up emotions and prevents harmful expressions of power.

If you have a need to control your child, most likely you have experienced too much helplessness in your own life. In playing these games you may experience healing for yourself as well. The need to control is out of your control, yet the choice to act or not to act on it can be yours. Once you can see the need to control as the weakness that it is, you will be able to feel powerful when you don't surrender to its grip. It takes emotional strength to flow with your child and not to yield to your impulses. In relating to children, your power comes from letting go and not from hanging on to your reactions.

Power games, such as those described above, have many faces and as parents we need to be on the alert, ready to spot them and to join in them. It is easy to tell the child to stop what he is doing; yet most of the time, when we are driven to say "stop," the child is initiating a creative game. It can be mashing up tofu, saying bathroom words, or throwing the Lego® blocks all over the floor just as soon as we finished picking them up. These invitations for power play need cooperative parents who say "Yes" when the mind wants to say "No." Instead of saying that the child is not cooperating, think of yourself as a player in his drama (which you are) and accept his invitation. In our home, when an adult does not respond to a child's playfulness, he or she is labeled "too serious" or "a pluff grownup." (Pluff: An Aldort family adjective meaning stuck in a stiff adult mode; lacking a sense of playfulness.) The child perceives the reserved adult as an obstacle to her creative or therapeutic play.

If we learn to take our own reactive thoughts less seriously, our children will learn to do the same. We don't have to obey our negating thoughts. We can, instead, flow with whatever the child is safely engaging us in. Doing so is what makes life peaceful and rich. We either struggle against the child's inclinations or we join his path with delight. Here is another example of a power game in which the child's action can be rejected or his invitation can be accepted, allowing him the sense of power:

> When Alex was about five years old his family lived in the country in a house that had no key. The glass door through which they entered the house could only be locked from the inside with a latch.
>
> One day, as the family was climbing up the stairs with bags of food in their hands, Alex sprang ahead of his parents and sister, entered the house, and locked the door. His parents saw his beautiful big eyes shining with excitement and anticipation behind the glass door.
>
> "Oh, no!" his father and mother exclaimed almost at once. "What are we going to do?" They put the bags of food on the porch's floor and started begging, "Oh please, let us in, oh please, please, the food will spoil." His older sister excitedly joined her parents in creating the theatrical scene.
>
> Alex was giggling with delight. He knew his parents were playing along and loved it. After a minute or so they escalated their plea with "Where will we

sleep? We are going to be cold. Oh no, what are we
going to do?" They started choosing sleeping spots and
acting frustrated with the discomfort that was await-
ing them.

They kneeled in front of the door again and begged
to be let in. After a couple of minutes Alex opened the
door with a victorious grin on his face. His parents and
sister walked in, expressing their gratitude, and bless-
ing the lucky day that the mighty Alex let them in.

This game occurred only a couple of times. After
that, Alex never did it again nor has he ever locked any
door in the face of anyone. His need was satisfied.

The declaration "Oh, no!" expressed dramatically and play-
fully can signal your participation in the game: When tofu is
turned into play-dough, you can gasp, "Oh no! What a mess."
When a child is drumming with her silverware, cover your ears
and say, "Oh no! What a noise." When you pick up the Lego®
blocks for the fourth time and your son spills them right over
again, exclaim, "Oh no! What are we going to do now?" as you
collapse on the floor. Any time safety is not an issue, just
replace "Stop" with a dramatic "Oh no!" and then accept the
offer of the game and play until the child directs you to stop it.
Although this may seem exhausting and time-consuming, it
actually takes less time to play along than to struggle against
the child. Of course, the long-term benefits will make your loving play worth thousands of happy moments with your child.
Besides, one important lesson children teach us is that the only
time is now, so enjoy it.

One pitfall to avoid when joining the child's power game is
the parent's tendency to become creative. Don't "steal" your
child's show. Accept his direction and only fill in the blank based

on his guidance. If you take over the leadership by introducing a twist that changes what he is doing, you are taking the power out of the child's hands. Save your gem and initiate a game some other time. Even when you initiate a game, let your child take over the direction it is going to take. At the same time, take your child's direction to its fullest expression. As long as you play the role he gave you, play it fully: be breathless, scared, desperate, and helpless in ways that fit the scene he creates.

As before, some parents may fear that their child will take advantage of them or that he won't respect them. Yet, the result of respecting your child and following his lead is that he will respect you more. Most often, a child who obeys does not respect his parents, but fears them. He may even despise them, and since he also loves them he may feel confused and ashamed of himself. He learns to control others and to see them as either one up or one down. Indeed, compliance is often not a sign of respect, but of fear and powerlessness. On the other hand, when you cooperate with your child, he learns to cooperate and to care for the needs of others. Children count on us to respond to their needs and it takes years and a lot of repetition before they give it fully back. Like learning to play a musical instrument or to dance, we cannot expect a few lessons to produce an accomplished performer.

Drawing and other artistic activities are valuable expressions of helplessness:

> *I recall counseling eight-year-old Georgia. She kept drawing her neighbor, whom she disliked and feared. She called her serial drawings "Valentina's Bad Day." The story went on over seven or eight*

*pages, describing one disaster after the other and cul-
minating in the neighbor burning in fire. Not only did
she draw it, but she then explained it to me with much
laughter, releasing her pent-up emotions.*

*I suggested that she keep telling her brother and par-
ents about "Valentina's Bad Day" as often as she wanted.*

*After about a week, Georgia was bored with her
drawings. To her mother's surprise, she went over to
Valentina who was working in the yard and
offered to help.*

*When she came back home, Georgia said, "Mom, I
helped Valentina plant some flowers. She is actually nice,
you know?" Georgia became more relaxed not only
around Valentina, but also in her relationships with
other people.*

The results of this art therapy showed up directly in the
relationship it was about. Often this is not the case. Sometimes
a child detests a neighbor, but his "hate" is really a manifestation of his fears about himself or about a family member. Doing
the therapy about the neighbor may do nothing to that relationship, but you may observe other positive changes in your
child's relationships, confidence, or other aspects of his life. Children use art, poetry, music, and a lot of acting and pretend games
to establish themselves as powerful. Cherish their creative healing methods and see them bloom.

Preventing Trouble When Away From Home

A bonus benefit to supporting a child's need to feel powerful is that it prevents problems from occurring away from home
and with other people. The other day I noticed a family who
left a restaurant in the middle of eating dinner because their

toddler had decided to throw the silverware and other items from the table to the floor and shriek with delight. The child's need for power and play was unleashed in the worst place for the parents.

Children whose need to control and feel powerful is satisfied at home can more easily enjoy and participate in activities in public. Make your home the place to let it all hang out and your child won't need to use your vulnerability in public to claim his power. At the same time, you must also respect your child's limitations in terms of self-restraint. Power games can be played before going to a concert, a restaurant, or a long ride. However, a restaurant may be the wrong place for some children and a fine place for others, especially if they had an opportunity to exude energy and feel in control before arriving there. Even a play group can be exciting for one child and an unbearable demand for another who may feel helpless and that she is failing in such a setting. Respecting the individual's needs and inclinations can go a long way toward preventing a sense of helplessness and its resulting defiance.

Interaction with other children is also affected by feelings of power or of helplessness. The child who often feels helpless may either become an unassertive follower or unleash his need for power by controlling or by disturbing other children. Give him a chance to experience being in control at home so he can enjoy his friends authentically.

In addition to playing power games, children derive a sense of power from being in charge of decisions and from being in charge of themselves. They occasionally feel empowered by helping in the home, but only when it is not required or

expected. When a child offers such help, express your gratitude and don't expect more. In addition, providing them safe
ways to be messy, noisy, as well as in charge, leads children to
contentment and healthy relationships. Life with children flows
when we simply follow their lead and respect their choices,
rather than wrack our brains for what we think is right for them.

By not depriving children of their power, I do not mean that
you give them license to do whatever they want. Like adults,
children live in a world that sets its own physical and social
boundaries. We need to be authentic with children so they live
a real life and not a fantasy life in which all their wishes are
promptly fulfilled. Natural frustrations that are not imposed
by anyone are a healthy part of growing up and you need only
to validate the child's feelings and listen.

A baby has no understanding of gravity, yet he does respond
to the limits it imposes on him; his falls are his training not only
for walking, but also for withstanding trials and errors. Likewise, a baby provides very little consideration for other people's
needs, which is the way it is supposed to be. His acquisition of
awareness and responsiveness to other beings grows over years
of being cared for in kind and generous ways, not by getting
his way at the expense of others. We reveal more social norms
to the child as he becomes ready to understand and to be
included in them. You cannot say to a baby, "I am too tired to
nurse you right now," and let him cry. Yet, within a couple of
years you can say, "Do you feel impatient because you want
the ice cream now? After dinner we will have ice cream with
our guests."

The tendency of loving parents to "make the child happy" by all means does not support the child's autonomy and emotional strength but weakens it. Love and nurture him and say yes to his autonomous choices, but avoid rescuing him from safe natural and social life lessons.

Physical Play

Physical play can either be a joy and an effective therapy or it might intensify a child's feelings of helplessness. Most of the time youngsters seem to enjoy physical rowdiness and gain physical and emotional competency from their rough play. Listen to children as they play and you will sometimes hear screams followed by crescendos of giggling. Most of the time you are not needed, and if you are concerned you can check things without being seen. When you have doubts you can ask a question to elicit information. Most often, the child you are concerned about will say something like "It's just a game, Mom. We're having fun." You can remind the more vulnerable child that you are available if things don't feel right for him. If your relationship with your children is one of trust, you can be sure that a child will call you when needed.

However, if you are concerned about a child's safety during any encounter, follow your intuition and check on the situation. With emotionally thriving children, the chances are that they will play safely and considerately; nonetheless, oppression does occur between youngsters. I have counseled adults who were intimidated, abused, and molested by siblings and have no idea why their parents never found out about it.

A mother called me because she was worried when she found out that her six-year-old son was locked in the closet by a new friend while the adults were visiting in the other room. Being in a strange house, the child was too intimidated to voice his fear, yet feeling safe with his mother, he told her about it afterwards.

A child who feels powerful has no need to resort to destruction or to bullying, yet a child who feels incompetent or helpless very well might, especially if he has no safe means of expressing himself. Sometimes we are surprised to find that our peaceful and loved child is violating the physical rights of a sibling or a friend:

> One day, abruptly and out of character, nine-year-old Jeremy started forcing his younger brother to the floor and restraining his movement. He kept doing so daily in spite of his brother's overt dislike of it. His mother, Martha, was baffled; Jeremy was a gentle child. She had no idea what the cause could be since she and her husband had never overpowered him. She sat him down daily to talk it over and try to understand his motive.
>
> "Do you get a sense of power out of restricting your brother?" Martha asked him in one of their conversations.
>
> "I don't know," Jeremy answered. "I can't control myself."
>
> "I know. But, what do you get out of it that feels satisfying?" Martha went on.
>
> Jeremy became silent and seemed lost inside himself. When he raised his glance, there was a smile of victory on his face as he announced, "I figured it out." He told his mother that he had been overpowered by a bigger boy at day camp and his need to force his brother

to lie under him started on that day. Jeremy's self-analysis was clear enough to help him see, with remorse, what he had been doing to his brother. While talking about the camp incident, Jeremy voiced considerable fear.

"I was so scared, Mom," he said, "and I felt ashamed to be so weak."

"Was the boy who forced you to the ground bigger than you?" Martha asked with much love in her voice.

"Yes. He was big and I felt so small."

Martha kept listening and showing understanding.

As a result of talking about his feelings with his mother's attention and validation, Jeremy no longer needed to overpower his brother.

Any time your child begins picking on someone younger than himself, check to see if he is feeling fearful as a result of experiences at home or elsewhere. Being controlled or scared can provoke aggressive behaviors as a means of regaining some measure of power and self-respect. To put an end to harmful physical displays of power, pay close attention to your child; show interest in his life away from home as well as at home with visitors and family members. Listen to him attentively. Help him express his feelings by asking validating questions, such as: "Would you like to be able to wear your sister's clothes whenever you want?" "Do you want to play with her your way?" "Were you scared when she threatened you?" Provide ways for your child to have an impact over his situation, play power games with the young, and give an older child the opportunity to share his feelings and to be in charge.

Adults have a hard time getting along; so do children. Don't expect your children to get along for longer than they can. To prevent some of your children's rivalry, provide for each child's need for attention, food, and focused activities. A child who is aggressive or annoying of other children is feeling helpless or is starving for power; you would be kind to offer him your attention. You can read him a book, play a power game, go for a walk together with all the children, or join their game.

Trusting children does not mean neglecting them. As long as we avoid taking sides and we don't take power away from them, we can contribute and offer our care as needed. When parents tell me (in private sessions and in workshops) how they were abused, tickled, and demeaned by their siblings, they always wish that their parents had intervened. Children do sometimes cause serious harm to each other; we are more likely to prevent such occurrences when we meet each child's basic emotional needs and when we are present in their lives.

We don't need to put children's emotional strength to the test and leave them playing together beyond their abilities. You wouldn't want to be overpowered by a "friend" and have your loving spouse be in the other room doing nothing. Children deserve our protection and they count on us to provide that. They assume that if we don't do anything, it means that the way they are treated is right. Prevent social settings that don't work, and meet each child's need for attention and focused activities, so play together is not an overload, but a good time for all.

Tickling

Tickling is typically initiated by adults, yet most people don't like to be tickled, and we certainly wouldn't tickle another adult.

Why then do we think that children enjoy it? In truth, children hate to be tickled, unless they have power over the tickling game, which means that they choose it and control its way and duration. If an adult tickles while the child has no say, the child does not like it. It violates his body just like any physical pain and not unlike hitting. The uncontrollable laughter it gives rise to is not a free expression of joy. If in fact the child could catch his breath, his laughter would be mingled with screams of "Stop it!" "No!" or "Enough!" Sometimes tickling reduces a child to such helplessness that he cannot say a word. As mentioned before, feeling helpless will cause the child to express his distress through aggression or in other destructive ways. In addition to the pain of being tickled, the child is learning from his experience to violate the body of another and to succumb to violation of his own body.

Although most children, having the choice, are unlikely to want to be tickled, on occasion a child may enjoy a tickling game, but only when he does not lose his power. I witnessed joy in a tickling game only once. This was when a three-year-old asked her mother to touch her under her arm. She then raised her elbow and Mom gently swept the back of her finger across her daughter's armpit for a second, stopping immediately as the child pulled away. Giggling, the child asked her mother to do it again. The girl was able to laugh because she was in charge and her mother was responsive to her. Such factors do not figure prominently in most tickling episodes, which more often than not render children helpless and are best avoided.

On another single occasion, a child told me about a tickling game which he liked. He and his two brothers would be on the bed and pushed each other off the bed by tickling. Like the game I witnessed, this game gave equal power and control to the three participants who could choose at will to withdraw and who were both the tickler and the tickled.

Wrestling

Parent-child wrestling does not teach children to be violent as long as they are not violated. When the parent retains the role of the underdog, it allows the child to fulfill the need to feel powerful. In fact, it is then a healing power game. If, however, a parent overpowers a child and holds him down, lifts him without his consent, tickles him, controls him, or otherwise evokes feelings of helplessness, the child is apt to express his frustration by imitating his parent's behavior, overpowering a younger person just as it was done to him or displaying other symptoms of distress.

Life affords children plenty of experiences of feeling helpless and we need not add to them. Your role is to give the child a chance to feel autonomous and to learn from you how a strong person treats a weaker one kindly.

The Compliant Child

Not all children express their feelings of helplessness through power games or aggression. Some tend to be more compliant, hoping to gain their parents' approval and avoid their anger. They internalize their sense of powerlessness, which can then manifest in depression, learning difficulties, sickness, or other physical, emotional, or behavioral difficulties. It is therefore vitally important to give an obedient child opportunities to feel powerful and autonomous. She will respond to power games just as well once she trusts that she won't lose your approval.

Because a child who is intent on pleasing others is most likely insecure and afraid to externalize her frustrations, she needs to experience herself as loved when she is not being compliant. She needs to regain freedom to choose to please you not from fear of losing your approval, but from her authentic desire to do so. To gain that freedom, the compliant child must experience herself as worthy and capable not only while pleasing you, but especially while simply being herself, and while defying you.

> *Ten-year-old Miranda had a habit of saying "Yes" when she wanted to say "No." After their session with me, her parents realized that their praise of her cooperation and their high expectations left her feeling insecure and too timid to assert herself. They became concerned and wanted to encourage her to feel her own power and assert herself. They started by telling Miranda about their own helpless moments so she would not feel isolated with her feelings. They also became alert for any hints of defiance Miranda sublimated.*
>
> *One day, when they came back from the store with bags of food, Miranda's father asked her if she would help put the stuff away. She sighed and then said, "Oh, okay."*
>
> *Her father saw the opportunity and said, "You hesitated; are you sure you want to help?"*
>
> *"It's all right. You need me to."*
>
> *"We can do it without you if you have other things you prefer to do right now."*
>
> *"Okay, then I want to go play now." Miranda looked at her father timidly and he smiled. "Good. Go play," he said, and she left to her room.*

One typical expression of helplessness in a docile child is a reluctantance to say "No." It is best not to ask your child to do things she is unlikely to enjoy doing. If you sincerely need her help, let her know what you need or ask her if she would like to give you a hand, but do accept "no" for an answer. If you notice a "yes" that is not sincere, reassure your child of your lack of expectation so she can feel free to be honest and assertive with you. She may help you very little, but when she does, it will be an authentic choice that will build her positive sense of herself. Acting on her choice to help freely, she will feel powerful rather than helpless and resentful, and therefore have a positive memory of helping. If you worry that she will never learn to do things that are not fun, keep in mind that everything becomes a joy when it is a free choice and vice-versa. Coercing children into doing housework against their will may be the reason so many adults detest doing chores.

In helping children satisfy their need to feel powerful and capable, our task is to be alert to both extroverted manifestations of helplessness (anger, aggression) and introverted ones (obedience, apathy, constant good behavior). The child who asserts herself and who takes a defiant action to fulfill her needs causes you to pay attention to her. The child who holds her feelings in needs you to reach out, converse, validate, and connect with her in ways that open the doors for her assertive expressions.

You must also find out how you have given your child the message that she will gain your approval through compliance and that asserting herself is not safe. Forgive yourself; you have been doing the best you can, and you are learning. If you used praise, rewards, threats, and/or disapproval, let her know that you have realized your error and you wish to stop using manipulation. Let her know that her autonomy and freedom are important to you. Show her your unwavering love unconditionally when she dares to step outside your expectations and at all other times.

The Development of Self-Reliance

A child feels powerful when he generates his own experiences. When we "rescue" him from certain experiences we consider "a failure," we rob him of the ownership of his power. Get out of the way so your child can plow his own field. He may have to do it many times before he gets what he wants, yet he will develop self-confidence and a trust in his own power. Strength is not the result of constant success but of the ability to withstand failure and move on again and again.

For many parents it is uncomfortable to see their children go through frustration or to let their children make their own, seemingly unwise, decisions. They assume that by helping the child to make his endeavor a success, they build his self-esteem and generate good feelings. Yet, self-esteem comes from the self and not from another. Unasked-for help, therefore, is in essence insulting and damaging to the child's sense of power and to the development of self-reliance.

If children are ever going to make responsible choices, they need to practice. This does not mean that you watch your child destroy his own dream, project, or well-being. Giving information can be done respectfully as long as we respond to the child's inquiry and don't take his project upon ourselves. After he has the information or knows how to get it, he needs to exercise his power by choosing his own direction. The trials and errors are his, with no room for blaming or victimizing; likewise, he also owns his triumphs fully.

From the time your children are babies, you can keep reminding yourself: Avoid helping your child unless you are asked. The tower of bricks may fall if your child puts one more block on; a friendship may end if your child insists on going through with a screwy plan; your child may not get into the science fair without your assistance with his project. Unless your child specifically asks for your input, it is best not to save the tower from falling, to keep the friendship from ending, to make sure the science project succeeds. And, when asked, respond only to what the child is inquiring. It is better not to build a new tower for him, suggest how to heal a friendship, or take over the science project. You can share your feelings but do what your child requests and no more. Even offering help with a question—"Would you like some information about the way this works?"—can be experienced as an insult for some children. You can offer to share your insight if you know that your child does not hesitate to reject it.

Although we adults have been around longer, a young human deserves to walk his own path. Our experience cannot be a way for him to leap over his own journey. We don't need to withhold information if asked for, yet we need to trust the child to use it or not use it. When his errors lead to disappointment or hurt, your confidence in his emotional resilience will be the greatest support you can provide, as Mary did for two-year-old Rhys:

Mary recalled the look on Rhys's face as he fell while running. She didn't move to pick him up; she didn't say a word. He looked up at her and she smiled calmly saying nothing. He then smiled, got up, and went on with his run.

A year later, Rhys fell off his tricycle. Mary saw it from the window; the tricycle landed on top of him and he burst out with a scream. She leaped toward the glass door but stayed inside the house unnoticed yet watching attentively to see if he needed her. In a few seconds he was through crying, got up, pulled the tricycle up, and rode away.

A child can feel free to generate his own feelings when we don't put ours in front of him. Likewise, predicting outcomes can be just as disempowering. Well-intentioned warnings like "Be careful, you could fall," "It could be dangerous," "It might not work out" or "I don't think you'll like it" may scare your child away from taking chances and from trusting himself. You can give factual information like "The ice is slippery," "This is hot and heavy," or "I am not sure they allow bare feet in the restaurant," but as long as his well-being is not in danger, let your child make his own decisions.

Children frequently take the path of greatest resistance in order to challenge themselves and accomplish more. Let your child learn that no matter the circumstances, he has the wherewithal to cope with life. Let him learn about life from his own experiences.

Chapter Six

❧

Self-Confidence

You are the mirror wherein your child sees his own worth

Sometimes, in spite of our devotion to meeting all their needs, children feel insecure about our love and about their own worth. To understand insecurity, you may want to examine your own moments of feeling intimidated, such as when you don't dare talk to someone, when you don't follow your inclination to do something, or when someone's tone of voice or choice of word leaves you doubting yourself. What is the conversation you hear in your head at such times? Or, when you are being evaluated or put on the spot, what does your mind say? Some common phrases are "I can't do it," "I am so stupid," "I will look ridiculous," "She won't like me," or "I am just not good enough," along with other words and phrases that undermine your confidence in yourself. These phrases are likely to be conclusions you have made as a child in response to your parents or they may be your parents' or siblings' own words recorded in your mind from years ago. These old phrases spring out inside your head automatically and result in self-doubt in the present.

For example, if your father always pointed out your imperfections, you are likely to make up a phrase that reflects feeling "not good enough." If your mother said, "I can't believe you did this," you could have translated it as "I can't do anything right." When these words are spoken in your mind, a set of feelings follows automatically.

The flip side of these statements are phrases that imply the same low view of one's self by pointing the finger at the other person in defensiveness: "Something is wrong with him," "He is such a jerk," or "Why can't she ever do anything right?" Such expressions allow the mind to relieve the sense of inadequacy by focusing on someone else's "faults."

You made up your self-image out of your parents' words, their facial expressions, and their treatment of you. If they honored who you were, you saw yourself as worthy; if they trusted your ability and your direction, you saw yourself as capable and self-reliant; yet if they criticized and controlled you, you may have wondered if you were really worthy of care and love.

Your child's inner messages of self-worth are made mostly of your relationship with him. If you carry old, self-doubting voices in your head, in spite of your best efforts, those old phrases that hurt you can fall on your child's ears and evoke similar emotions.

Building self-esteem starts in the womb. Wanting the child and making this want known moment by moment is the foundation of confidence. The baby assumes he is worthy of your love and care. He seems to take it for granted, which is evident in his assertiveness and in his dismay and rage when you don't care for him for even a moment. To keep that confidence intact, simply respond to your baby's needs promptly and joyfully. A denial of his expressed needs can become the foundation of self-doubt, while your delight and responsiveness will preserve his self-confidence. When his choices to nurse, move, rest, sleep, or play are met with expressive joy and affection, he will move on confidently to the next stage. When he sees the spark of excitement in your eyes in response to his being and your delight in serving him, he will conclude, "I am worthy."

As his power to engage in the world expands dramatically, the toddler needs more of your confidence in him to support his courageous experiments. The child then feels confident because his choices get your vote of confidence and not because he succeeds in everything. Be present and join his joys and sorrows so he learns to feel comfortable with the many experiences of being alive. He will not be afraid to assert himself and to try new things when he feels equally comfortable with failure and with success. Instead of giving praise and using other manipulations, embrace his direction with curiosity and with delight. Keep in mind, however, that there is no lifetime guarantee for self-esteem. Even when we provide for all of a child's emotional and physical needs in his early years, insecurity may show up periodically and require our attention.

The Building Blocks of Self-Confidence

A child's spirit can shrivel without actual verbal abuse; it is the more subtle ways of diminishing the child's sense of self that often escape our scrutiny. The following general guidelines can help you focus on your child's sense of confidence and self-worth:

- Help your child only when she asks and only as much as she asks. Uninvited help is likely to cause her to conclude that she is incapable, because the silent message she receives from you is "I don't think you can do this on your own. You need my help. You are not capable."
- Provide your child with the freedom to try things on her own even when you know that she cannot do them (as long as she is safe and, when not, provide an alternative). Grant her the opportunity to fail or err. She will learn from such personal experience that she is strong and capable in the face of difficulties and that she can rely on herself. Successful people are not those who never fall, but those who keep getting up after their falls; instead of feeling fear, they feel comfortable with falls and inspired to keep going.
- Support a child's choices without expecting specific results. Accept outcomes with neutrality, and emotional expressions with respect and care. You can validate her frustration, joy, or disappointment, but keep your opinion about her actions to yourself or at least make sure it doesn't sway her away from her own convictions: "My view is different and I enjoy seeing you going on your own path."
- Express gratitude and avoid correcting or criticizing your child's actions. For example, if your child offers to sweep the floor and you then redo the sweeping, she is unlikely to offer her help again and will see herself as incapable or even clumsy. If she has mowed the lawn and Dad expresses dissatisfaction because it's a little uneven, or if her spelling or reading errors are pointed out when she didn't ask for it, the child's self-esteem and development will undoubtedly

suffer. A child who makes an effort to do something helpful needs to hear only gratitude, not evaluation, and one
who learns new skills needs trust and sometimes acknowledgment, not criticism. She will improve her abilities with
time, provided that she feels good about herself and receives
the learning tools she asks for (classes, books, tools, feedback, etc.).

- Avoid praise and instead mirror the child's expressed feelings and share in her joy. Praising children for behaviors
("You are so helpful, Johnny!") and achievements ("I'm so
proud you won first place in the Cub Scout contest!") causes
them to do things for the sake of getting the kudos rather
than for their own sake. A child may do anything to win
your praise and may become dependent on external
approval and achievement-based acceptance. Thus, ironi-
cally, praise and rewards can lower a child's self-esteem
just as surely as criticism can.[1]

- Let go of your agenda for the child, and cherish her exactly
the way she is. Expressing expectations, as in "Say 'Hi' to
Aunt Judy," can leave the child feeling inadequate, especially if she forces herself to comply with your wishes. Even
achievements must be the child's agenda, not yours. If you
say, "You will be such a great athlete," a child may fear
that she could not live up to your standards and give up, or
she may devote herself to athletics to please you; she may
then lose her authentic motivation or even her passion. It is
therefore best to avoid making suggestions or creating
expectations for achievement. Your joy in who the child is
and in her point of view is a vote of confidence that is by far

more likely to preserve her natural motivation to excel. (This is different than the relationship between a student and a teacher. The teacher inspires the student to reach high standards in a field that the student chooses and elects that teacher to coach her.)

- As much as possible, avoid negating your child's expressions and direction. Saying "no" too often or contradicting the child's ideas can wilt her assurance in herself because she may conclude, "My choices seem to be the wrong ones. I can't trust myself." Even if she can't have what she wants, her choice is still valid and worthy of consideration.

- Avoid comparing your child to anyone else. Comparison with others creates a sense of competition and a fear of losing, regardless of which side of the comparison the child is on.

- Allow your child the burden of responsibility based on her readiness and interests. When you do everything for her, selecting what she should wear, suggesting what she should do, or reminding her of tasks and obligations (when not asked to), you undermine her sense of responsibility, fostering a loss of self-reliance. By being responsible for her own choices and actions, your child will develop a sense of self-trust.

- Listen to your child and validate her emotional expressions. Her self-esteem will grow from knowing that her feelings and how she expresses them are valued.

- Respect your child's knowledge and wisdom. If she asks a question, don't turn your response into a lecture or a test. A request for information that turns into a test or a lesson often leaves the child feeling humiliated or bored and therefore less willing to inquire again. She will share her knowledge and interest with you more often when you don't probe and teach.

• Treat your child as your equal, which she is. Equal does not mean the same. She lacks experience and deserves to have her limitations respected as well as enjoyed. Entering life later than someone else does not render anyone less worthy or deserving of full respect. Your child is always doing the best she can, just like you.

• Spilled milk is not an invitation for criticism, but for help in cleaning it up. When your child makes a mistake, stay neutral or helpful. Use S of S.A.L.V.E. to Separate your inner monologue from the present occurrence, so you can focus on what is needed in the present (you can investigate your thoughts later for your own sake). If your child is upset, listen, validate, and reassure her of your love and appreciation. If she does something that seems to you stupid or clumsy, keep the criticism to yourself (it is material for your own self-discovery) or reflect on her feelings; she may be pleased with herself or she might feel embarrassed, angry, or confused. If she expresses self-doubt, you can validate and tell her about the stupid or clumsy things you've done so she knows that such things happen to everybody and are part of being human.

• Devote time to your child. If she is too young to endure waiting, interrupt your activity and be with her excitedly. If she is old enough to wait and you cannot spend time with her when she asks you to, let her know how soon you will be able to join her. Then, show up on time and be a focused and engaged companion. If on a regular basis you tell your child "I have no time to do this with you" or "I'll play with you later," she will see herself as unimportant.

- When you are with your child, follow her lead and participate in her world respectfully. You can lead when she asks you to. Make sure she knows how happy you are to be with her.

- When your child asks for assistance, respond as promptly as you can and with a joyful spirit. If, on a regular basis, she sees an expression of impatience on your face or if you speak to her with irritation in your voice, she might conclude that she is a nuisance to you.

The above suggestions apply to any relationship at any age. You won't be likely to need this list for your relationships with friends and colleagues, as you treat them in this manner anyway. In our culture, however, many of the respectful ways we use with adults do not seem to be carried on with children. If you don't remember some of this guidance, you can always ask yourself, "How would I respond in this situation if this were an adult I revere?"

Anxieties about "How will she ever learn?" or "She will take advantage of me" come from our past, projected as fear into the future. These are grist for the mill of our personal development (investigate these thoughts later with S of S.A.L.V.E.) and have nothing to do with the child. Be here now with your child and you will know how to honor who she is and to cherish the moment with her. Listen to who she is rather than to voices from your past and pressures from friends and family. Your delight in the child will result in her self-esteem.

What Self-Confidence Is and Isn't

Sometimes people mix up confidence with being outgoing. Children can be confident in themselves without being outgoing. It is crucial to distinguish between our own emotional interpretations and the actual self-esteem of the child. An introverted child who prefers privacy and refuses to converse with adults about his age and knowledge may not be insecure. On the contrary, he could be asserting himself in action; he is not feeling a need to appease the adult by behaving contrary to his inner voice. While adults don't approach another adult with such patronizing questions, they seem surprised when a child is confident enough to deny them the unauthorized investigation. In a similar way, a child who does not like to mingle with groups of children and prefers an intimate friendship with one or two is being confident when refusing to join a group game. He is being authentic and not intimidated by anyone's expectations of him.

> *I recall one of my children, at age four-and-a-half, at a play day. Several children were engaged in play with parents. He sat on the side observing. I sat with him expecting to either sit there the whole time or go home if he requested so.*
>
> *The organizer of the event felt a need to include my son in the play. A couple of times she came over and tried to seduce him and convince him to play. He looked at her eyes and shook his head for "no." This boy has always known what he wants and he never inches away from his intent.*

On the other side of the spectrum of personalities there are children whose confidence shows up in clear, extroverted ways, such as in leadership or a desire to be on stage. Yet, not every outgoing child is confident. Sometimes a "me, me," character can be a cover-up for deep-seated insecurity. Indeed, even flamboyance can sometimes be a way of covering up insecurity or living up to expectations. Therefore, don't look for conventional features of confidence in your child; rather, ask yourself whether he is true to himself. If he loves the stage or is a natural leader, loud, or entertaining, then such behaviors are authentic expressions of who he is. If, however, he acts in response to your aspirations, it may not be confidence but insecurity that drives him. He may need to be encouraged to follow his own passions and inspiration. For instance, ten-year-old Iris was an insecure child who was loud and always at the head of the line:

> Iris always shouted "Me first!" at the beginning of each drama group activity. She jumped and got to the front of the line constantly. She seemed very happy when she got to be noticed and to be first, but easily upset if she wasn't.
>
> Coming home from one drama class, Iris acted aggressive with her sister, Andrea, and was generally irritable. Her mother was puzzled. "Becky said you had such fun at acting class today, yet you came back and you seem upset."
>
> "I didn't have a good time. She never calls on me. I hate her," Iris said.
>
> Mom said nothing. Later, she was sitting at the piano with Andrea. Iris passed by and said on the run, "Ah, little genius Andrea, do no harm."

What looks like confidence and exuberance, in this situation, is really Iris's despair and insecurity. She is jealous at home and in her anguish she tries to negate her self-doubt by looking for recognition everywhere she goes.

Here are additional examples of confident behavior in relatively quiet and shy children:

> *When my oldest son, Yonatan, was six, he chose to take part in a summer art class. When I arrived to pick him up at the end of the class, I looked into the room and Yonatan wasn't there. To my astonishment the teacher said that Yonatan had been disturbing the class and that she had sent him to the secretary's office upstairs.*
>
> *As I started toward the stairs I heard my son's cheerful voice on his way down, talking happily to the secretary. When Yonatan saw me he said, "I had a great time, Mom. I played with Tina in the office."*
>
> *"Why did you go to the office?" I asked.*
>
> *"I was painting a picture and the teacher disturbed me. She wanted me to stop and listen to a story and she said that after the story I would be doing another picture. I wanted to keep painting the first picture so she said to go to the office. I don't want to go to the art class again. I can paint at home without interruptions."*

Self-confidence is the result of feeling important and deserving of the best. Sometimes adults see confident behavior in children as rude and miss the opportunity to celebrate the child's assertiveness. If we can recognize the child's courage to assert her will, we can be on her side and nurture this growing confidence. Here is another story about Yonatan, which illustrates confidence that comes from seeing himself as deserving:

> *Eight-year-old Yonatan was busy playing outside with the water hose. His father became concerned about the waste of water and called to him from inside the*

house, "Please shut the water off. The well can run out of water."

Not hearing his father, Yonatan went on playing, at which point his father became angry. He went to the window and shouted, "Shut that water off right now!"

Stunned, Yonatan quickly turned off the spigot and ran into the house. When he faced his father, his eyes were brimming with tears and his face red with anger.

"If I shouted at you 'Go shut the door of your van right now!' how would you feel?" he asked.

"I would feel hurt," Dad answered and apologized; they clarified the misunderstanding and discussed ways to prevent such hurts in the future.

Some people may feel shocked by this boy's words to his father. Yet, his expression indicated that he felt confident and safe. Such openness is the result of feeling secure. Yonatan reflected on his thought, "How can you treat me this way? I am worthy of being treated well, just like you." Children who feel safe are free to express their feelings and have an implicit sense of their own worthiness.

Furthermore, Yonatan's freedom to express himself, combined with his father's respect, healed his resentment spontaneously. If his dad had preached to him or inhibited his self-expression, the boy might have become angrier, escalating the conversation into an unpleasant encounter. As a result, he might have deepened his resentment and resorted to lying or suppressing his feelings the next time a similar incident occurred. In demonstrating respect and empathy, his father gave himself and his son the chance to heal and to forgive.

What makes such family interactions possible is a child's absence of fear in day-to-day relationships. He knows that

whatever feelings and thoughts he may have are taken seriously. He feels deserving of the time, attention, and respect he
receives. Yonatan is now a young man who can listen to
someone's rage, validate feelings, and stay completely centered
and calm.

The paradox is that often we worry that something is wrong
with a child who is confident. We want him to be assertive and
secure, but when he is, we may get uptight, wanting to dampen
his spirit. If your child stands up for himself in the face of adult
condescension, you have a reason to celebrate, even when the
adult is you.

Self-Esteem and Siblings/Peers

The arrival of a new sibling can be an extremely heart-
wrenching experience for a young child, shaking her confidence
in her own worth. She may be excited and loving, yet also shocked
and heartbroken. A mother I counseled confided to me that she
remembers the arrival of her baby sister as the most traumatic
event in her life. She was a four-year-old then; she felt as though
life was coming to a tragic end for her. She thought she had "lost
the battle" and was replaced by someone better. My oldest son,
Yonatan, put it best when I was pregnant with our second child:
"Why do you want another Yonatan?" he asked.

All the parental preparations seem to vanish in the face of
the reality of the new sibling. Your child may wish to return to
the days of being your only child or the youngest one. To fully
understand what a child may feel upon the arrival of a new sibling, put yourself in her place. Imagine your spouse bringing

home another partner (wife/husband) with great and obvious excitement. The explanation is logical; you two are so happy together, and you are so wonderful, why not have more happiness with another partner?[2]

Take this image beyond the initial shock and go with it as far as possible into images from daily life. Taking turns, watching your lover enjoying the other partner, being expected to share with delight, and asked to be a close and loving friend to that person. Imagine an actual scenario that fits your family and the kind of things you do and places you go. Put the new partner at the dinner table, in bed, on vacation; picture that person hiking, cooking, hugging, expressing affection, and sharing your own special kind of moments. I am sure (with rare exceptions) that you are getting in touch with some very unpleasant emotions. If you are deeply into it, you may feel literally sick and overwhelmed. You may feel helpless, fearing there is no solution to this situation other than getting rid of the "invader," which is what children often feel and fantasize about siblings.

Many children respond lovingly when the sibling is an infant; as soon as she moves around just like them, the delayed shock settles in and they start showing signs of stress. They realize that this is not just a baby, not just a "toy" for them to have, but another whole person. Now they have to share toys, parental attention, and ice cream with their "rival."

How a child responds to having a sibling varies greatly from child to child and depends on age. Most older children, seven and up, respond well to a new sibling, but if a child is young enough to still need similar attention to the kind a baby receives, she is likely to have a difficult time accepting the newcomer. A young child fears that she is not worthy and that the baby will replace her, while an older child looks forward to taking care of the young arrival.

In the nuclear family there is only one of each parent. The moment there is another child, the scarcity of adult caregivers often creates tension. Competition and self-doubt make themselves at home as though they came attached to the new child. Who is better and who gets more attention and love becomes the measure of one's worth. The challenge of sibling rivalries is not a bad situation to be avoided, simply one to be aware of, so it can provide an opportunity for growing and not for wilting. The key to empowering your child in the face of a new sibling is your awareness of her possible experience and your ability to stay connected and delighted with her.

Some parents believe they can prevent this tension between siblings. With grandparents or other help they may be able to do so to some degree. In most families, however, this process is not preventable. Parents usually take action only after the older child already exhibits signs of distress and shriveling self-esteem, because these symptoms seem to show up all at once. Parents often tell me, "We don't have any problems like this. Our children love each other." Yet, often, one day one child starts hurting the other and the surprised parents call me for guidance.

When a child becomes aggressive toward her sibling or toward you, when she is whining, clingy, raging, or regressing, or when she shows any other signs of distress you think is related to having a sibling, she is already feeling desperate. She worries that you don't love her anymore and that she may be worthless. If you try to stop her expressions of distress, she concludes that she is bad and worthless indeed. "Mom stops me from hurting the baby. She protects the baby. The baby is good. I must be bad." Her resentment toward her sibling then grows in leaps and bounds. The more you try to teach her gently to be kind and loving, the lonelier she is with her distress, which is far from feeling gentle or loving. She may wish to reverse her fate and may fantasize getting rid of her sibling. She then feels guilty and undeserving and so the vicious cycle can get very painful and her behavior gets worse as her self-image deteriorates and her anguish rises.

To assist a child through such a challenging passage, avoid scolding her and instead validate her feelings. My middle child, Lennon, had a hard time accepting his younger brother. Here is his story:

> *Five-year-old Lennon used to be loving and gentle with his one-year-old brother. One day, out of the blue, he started snatching toys out of his little brother's hands, and he looked satisfied when the baby, Oliver, cried. Initially we encouraged Lennon to be gentle and tried to teach him to understand that Oliver doesn't like it. Lennon became even more aggressive. I realized that Lennon needed more than gentle reminders.*
>
> *The next time this happened, instead of asking Lennon to stop, I gave him a hug and said, "Do you wish that it would be just you and me, without Oliver, the way we were before?"*
>
> *Lennon looked uncomfortable and said nothing. He expected a preaching that fit with his self-image of the "bad" one.*
>
> *"I miss being with you too," I said.*
>
> *"No you don't," Lennon whispered.*

"So, when you see me holding the baby all the time, do you feel lonely?"

Lennon nodded.

"And then you tell yourself that Mom doesn't care about you?"

I took him into my arms and said, "I miss being just with you so much. I love you all the time. When I hold Oliver, I love you."

Lennon looked down and I was sensing that he was feeling guilty and undeserving of my love because he may be having violent fantasies about his brother.

"Would you like to throw the baby in the garbage?" I asked.

Lennon perked up. "Yes," he said, and we took an imaginary baby to the garbage.

"Would you like to show me what else you want to do to Oliver? Here is a doll." (Dad was with Oliver and Yonatan in the other room, so he was not exposed to his brother's fantasy play.)

After Lennon played out some of his fantasies I said, "I know how you feel. It is fine to have these thoughts. Next time you feel like this, come and show me what you want to do to Oliver. I love knowing how you feel and what you imagine, and you can always show me with the doll."

The next time Lennon bothered his brother I again offered him to show me with the doll (in the other room) what he wanted to do to Oliver. He did and we kept doing this as needed. Three days later, Lennon, of his own volition, came to me when he was ready to annoy his brother. Instead of annoying him, he said, "Mom, let me show you what I want to do to Oliver."

He went with me to the other room and showed me, and by doing so he prevented himself from hurting the real Oliver. He kept doing so. Two weeks later he asked me to come with him to do the fantasy with the

doll, but instead of playing out the fantasy of hurting
Oliver, he wanted to take the doll and do with it things
that make Oliver laugh and enjoy himself. That was
the end of his aggression toward his brother.

By validating and playing the doll game I did not dramatize Lennon's story nor claim that it was real. I did just the opposite; I let him know that I love him no matter who is in my arms, that I miss time alone with him, and that my love keeps growing. I let him know with my attitude and confidence that I trust his inner power to overcome this painful phase. We discussed it openly. He was depressed and asked me if there was a homeopathic remedy for wanting to hurt his brother. Lennon really didn't want to hurt Oliver; he wanted very much to regain his peace and sense of worth — and he did.

In addition to the power of validation and acceptance, it is crucial that each child has one-on-one time with Mom and Dad. The nuclear family makes Mom and Dad rare commodities to compete for. There will be less competition and tension when each child's need for attention is satisfied.

Yet, no matter how much you succeed in this acrobatic dance of meeting your children's needs, you are bound to relax when things are good and then have to quench fires again and again. Sibling tensions will ebb and flow, reflecting the children's self-esteem and the dynamics of your family. Therefore, enjoy the calm times, but be on your toes for repeat flares of distressed behavior so you can take care of the child's need before her stress level causes lasting damage to her self-esteem.

As siblings grow older together, the ebbs and flows of their relationships become part of life. Just like adults, they go through peaceful periods followed by struggles and insecurity. Most of the time a child whose self-esteem is repeatedly threatened by a sibling, friend, or another relative needs time with a loving parent so she can rebuild her belief in herself. This may mean sending the older sibling (if old enough) to Grandma's for a day, separating the children's rooms, or providing new activities with you or with other playmates whereby the child gets to experience herself as a valued person. Increase the opportunities for each child to create her individual path whereby she is not competing or sharing with her sibling, and make your connection with each child an individual one. No one feels loved in pairs or groups.

The only obstacle to self-esteem is a thought that tells the child she is not worthy. She has a story that is the evidence to her worthlessness or failure. Take her proofs away and her story will crumble. If you tell her not to hurt the baby, she has a proof that she is bad and that you don't love her (you protect the baby from the bad girl). You can deflate her drama by hugging her while she wants to hurt her brother, by validating her need, and by providing supportive outlets for her fantasies. When you fight her you enforce her pain; when you join her on her quest, she will go with you into your story of love.

Demeaning Amongst Siblings

As the children grow older, they may start using demeaning remarks toward a sibling as a way to feel worthy. These hostile interactions may be benign and harmless, or they can hurt a child who takes them seriously. Feeling insecure and inferior may drive a child to fulfill his need by demeaning another child. As for the receiver of "insults," one child may get hurt by such interaction, while a self-assured child may not mind it much. You can find out how the child is feeling by observing and by asking.

The self-assured child can be unmoved by demeaning words while a child who is not as secure may become aggressive or express her hurt in words or other troubling behaviors. One father told me that when he asked his nine-year-old son what he felt when his sister called him a brat, he responded, "Nothing," and his behavior confirmed his indifference to her words. Therefore, much of what looks to parents as a painful exchange between children can be harmless and need no intervention. However, there are times when a child is being hurt by repeated put-downs, which means that he believes what is being said.

When you assess that your child is feeling hurt, empower her to connect with who she really is, so the words of her siblings will lose their power. Listen to her and avoid implying that her sibling's words control her feelings. Saying "He makes you feel..." implies that her feelings are controlled by his words. On the contrary, after you listen to her, validate in a way that empowers her sense of self: "Would you like to feel good about yourself, regardless of your brother's opinions?" This can lead to her recognition of her virtues independently of anyone's words. Once she sees her own value inside herself, no one can take it away. She will learn that who she is, is unaffected by anyone's words.

While meeting the needs of the hurt child, make sure to validate her sibling's need to demean. Why does she need to demean her sister? Is she trying to prove herself better because she doubts herself? Does she doubt your love? Can she distinguish her painful thought from reality?

Self-doubt is never real, because each child is always a worthy and lovable human being. Look for specific needs that may be neglected. Meeting her needs for privacy, attention, love, and other specific interests will leave her satisfied so she won't need to unleash her frustration on a sibling.

If you find yourself siding with one child over the other, stop and listen to your inner conversation (S of S.A.L.V.E.), then turn your attention (A) to each child, listen (L) and validate (V) each one's feelings without favoring or criticizing either one. Listen to each child fully. Validating one child does not contradict doing the same for the other. We are not settling their dispute, only validating their feelings and acknowledging their preferences or point of view. Not intervening with the content empowers (E) the children to trust themselves and to be resourceful.

As you assess whether one of the children is hurt, you are likely to find that the "offender" is often in greater emotional need, as was the case with Aaron:

> *Seven-year-old Joseph came out of the playroom, crying, "Mom, Aaron is calling me a donkey and he ruined my tower."*
>
> *Rebecca hugged Joseph and said, "Are you a donkey?"*
> *"No. Mom, he broke my tower."*
> *"Would you like to rebuild it?"*
> *At this point twelve-year-old Aaron came out of the playroom. "Oh, is he complaining again like a baby to Mommy?" he said with a teasing tone of voice.*

Rebecca recognized the pain in Aaron's expression. She approached him, touched him, looked in his eyes, and asked, "Would you like to spend some time with me right now?"

Aaron sat by his mom on the couch. At this point Joseph, our original "victim," left the room and went back to play. He most likely felt cared for. His brother's pain was deeper.

"What's the worst thing about having a brother?" Rebecca asked Aaron. He perked up and started telling her all about it. She listened attentively and could hear Aaron's sense of failure. Her validation brought some tears and many little stories that clarified why he was feeling crushed by the presence of his younger brother in his life. It was Aaron's doubt in his own worth that drove him to annoy his brother.

In his phone session with me the next day, Aaron said to me, "I hate my brother."

"Would you prefer that he was gone?" I asked.

"Yes," he said.

"Tell me how it would feel at home without him," I said.

Aaron was silent. After a while he said, "No, I don't want him gone. I can't stand that thought."

"So, you do want your brother to live with you?"

"I guess. I can't imagine not having him. I do love him; it is just that he is such a nag."

"What kind of a nag? Tell me more."

"Oh, I don't know. He is really okay."

"Are you okay, Aaron?"

"I think I am. Yes. I wish my Mom had more time for me, and my Dad too. They spend so much time with Joseph."

"They don't spend time with you?"

"Well, no, they do, it's just that...well, I don't really want more time with them. He is younger. I don't need it. I need my time with friends."

"So your brother is really okay, your parents love you and spend the right amount of time with you. Any problems?"

Aaron was laughing. "I am sure I can make one up. It's amazing how I made up that story."

Our goal is not to accomplish the impossible task of raising children who never experience a blow to their self-image. Such a life does not exist, and shielding a child from real experiences will only weaken him. Instead, children need to grow up able to face reality with emotional strength and wisdom. We are seeking to build a loving and fear-free relationship with our children, one that allows for the expression of all emotions and lets our youngsters feel confident in their worth. This, in turn, bolsters the self-assurance they will need to build a meaningful life for themselves and to have a positive effect on others.

Support your child's sense of self-worth daily by affirming who she is, by voting "yes" for her direction, and by expressing your love and appreciation authentically. This means that there are no expectations to stand in the way of the joyous celebration of who the child is.

Notes: Chapter Six

1. See Aldort's articles on praise: "Mothering" #71 1994; "Life Learning" magazine Nov/Dec 02, Jan/Feb 03, Mar/Apr 03.
2. This analogy first introduced by Mazlish and Faber's book *Siblings Without Rivalry: How to Help Your Children Live Together So You Can Live Too*. HarperResource, 1998.

Suggested Sources

Books:

Blanton, B. *Radical Parenting*. Sparrow Hawk Publications, 2002.

Breeding, J. *The Wildest Colts Make the Best Horses*. Bright Books, 1996.

Breeding, J. *True Nature and Great Misunderstandings: On How We Care for Our Children According to Our Understanding*. Eakin Press, 2004.

Briggs, D. *Your Child's Self-Esteem*. Mainstreet Books, 1975.

Byron, Katie *Loving What Is: Four Questions That Can Change Your Life*. Harmony Books, 2002.

Byron, Katie *I Need Your Love: Is That True? How to Stop Seeking Love, Approval and Appreciation and Start Finding Them Instead*. Harmony Books, 2005.

Greenberg, D. *Free at Last: The Sudbury Valley School*. Sudbury Valley Press, 1995.

Greenberg, D. *Child Rearing*. Sudbury Valley Press, 1987.

Holt, J. *How Children Learn*. Perseus Publishing, Revised edition, 1995.

Holt, J. *How Children Fail*. Perseus Publishing, Revised edition, 1995.

Holt, J. *Instead of Education: Ways to Help People Do Things Better*. Sentient Publications, 2004.

Holt, J. *Learning All the Time*. Addison Wesley Publishing Company, Reprint edition, 1990.

Holt, J. *Never Too Late: My Musical Life Story*. Addison Wesley Publishing Company, Reprint edition, 1991.

Hunt, J. *The Natural Child: Parenting from the Heart*. New Society Publishers, 2001.

Juul, J. *Your Competent Child: Toward New Basic Values for the Family.* Farrar Straus Giroux, 1st American edition, 2001.

Kohn, A. *Unconditional Parenting: Moving from Rewards and Punishments to Love and Reason.* Atria, 2005.

Kohn, A. *Punished By Rewards: The Trouble with Gold Stars, Incentive Plans, A's, Praise and Other Bribes.* Mariner Books, 1999.

Kohn, A. *No Contest: The Case Against Competition.* Houghton Mifflin Company, 1987.

Leo, Pam *Connection Parenting.* Wyatt-MacKenzie Publishing, 2005

O'Mara, P. *Natural Family Living: The Mothering Magazine Guide to Parenting.* Atria, 2000.

Neill, A.S. *Summerhill: A Radical Approach to Child Rearing.* Hart (UK), 1984.

Neill, A.S. *Freedom - Not License!* Hart (UK), 1966.

Rosenberg, M, Ph.D. et al. *Nonviolent Communication : A Language of Life: Create Your Life, Your Relationships, and Your World in Harmony with Your Values.* Puddledancer Press, 2003

Thevenin, T. *The Family Bed.* Avery, 1987.

Winn, Marie *The Plug-In Drug: Television, Computers and Family Life.* Penguin, 2002.

Childbirth and Health Books:

Mendelsohn, R, M.D. *Male Practice.* Contemporary Books, 1981

Mendelsohn, R, M.D. *How to Raise a Healthy Child in Spite of Your Doctor.* Ballantine Books, 2001

Noble, E. *Childbirth with Insight.* Houghton Mifflin Co., 1983.

Journals and Magazines:

Life Learning (Canada): The International Magazine of Self-Directed Learning

Mothering: The Magazine of Natural Family Living

Byron Child (Australia): The Magazine for Progressive Families

Natural Parenting (Australia): Real Alternatives for Today's Parents

The Mother Magazine (United Kingdom)

Journal for Family Living

Compleat Mother: Magazine About Breastfeeding, Childbirth and Pregnancy.

Web Sites that Offer Opportunities for Self-Realization:

TheWorkForParents.com
AuthenticParent.com
NaomiAldort.com
TheWork.org
Landmarkeducation.com
Sedona.com
Radicalhonesty.com

Web Sites About Health for Children and Adults:

WestonAPrice.org
Mercola.com

Supportive Organizations:

La Leche League
Attachment Parenting International
Commercial Alert
The Natural Child Project
Nonviolent Communication

Contact Information

Naomi Aldort, Ph.D., is an internationally published parenting writer, speaker, and counselor who combines The Work with specific parenting guidance based on each parent's individual direction (attachment, unschooling, mainstream, etc.). She uses the process of inquiry to reveal the thoughts and beliefs that obstruct a parent's ability to act from love.

Naomi's articles and advice columns can be found in publications worldwide, including *Mothering Magazine* (US), *The Journal of Attachment Parenting International*, a McGraw Hill's university textbook, *Byron Child* (AU), *Natural Parenting* (AU), *The Mother* (UK), *Hand in Hand* (US), *Life Learning Magazine* (CA), *Taking Children Seriously* (UK), *Gentle Spirit*, and more. Naomi's articles have been translated into German, Hebrew, Japanese, Spanish, and Dutch.

For more information, please visit Naomi's websites:

www.NaomiAldort.com
www.TheWorkForParents.com
www.AuthenticParent.com
(800) 747-7916
naomi@aldort.com
Naomi Aldort, Ph.D.
P.O. Box 1719
Eastsound, WA 98245

Naomi Aldort Products & Services

For more details: www.naomialdort.com

Audio Recordings

Trusting Our Children, Trusting Ourselves, a set of 7 CDs
Babies & Toddlers: To Tame or to Trust, a set of 2 CDs
The Price of Praise - 2 CDs

Phone Counseling

Naomi has many years of experience counseling parents worldwide. She uses The Work so you can discover your own power, wisdom, and peace in relating to your children. The Work is a simple process of inquiry into the thoughts that produce your stress, confusion, and misunderstanding of yourself, your children, and others. When you gain clarity, you find the answers to your difficulties to be self-evident and liberating, and your children thrive.

In addition, Naomi offers hands-on guidance on how to live with your child in a way that allows both of you to flourish authentically and in freedom.

Workshops/Speaking

Naomi offers the *Raising Our Children, Raising Ourselves* weekend workshop, as well as other workshops that cater to specific ages and interests. With Naomi's guidance, you will use The Work to propel yourself toward peace and freedom with your children, spouse, and others and discover the joy of parenting outside the old paradigm of uninvestigated thoughts.

Family Intensive Retreat

The Family Retreat is a private family workshop in Naomi Aldort's home or yours. It is an intense, life-transforming experience, with many counseling hours each day.

(800) 747-7916
naomi@aldort.com
Naomi Aldort, Ph.D.
P.O. Box 1719, Eastsound, WA 98245

Your children are not your children.

They are the sons and daughters of Life's longing for itself.

They come through you but not from you,

And though they are with you, yet they belong not to you.

You may give them your love but not your thoughts.

For they have their own thoughts.

You may house their bodies but not their souls,

For their souls dwell in the house of tomorrow, which you
  cannot visit, not even in your dreams.

You may strive to be like them, but seek not to make them
  like you.

For life goes not backward nor tarries with yesterday.

You are the bows from which your children as living arrows
  are sent forth.

The archer sees the mark upon the path of the infinite, and
  He bends you with His might that His arrows may go
  swift and far.

Let your bending in the archer's hand be for gladness;

For even as He loves the arrow that flies, so He loves also
  the bow that is stable.

- From *The Prophet*
by Kahlil Gibran

Oliver Aldort

"Anybody who expected the Saint-Saens Cello Concerto No.1 to be a mere novelty would have been more than surprised. Oliver Aldort may have just turned 11, he may be slightly shorter than his cello, but he already has a remarkable technique, impeccable intonation and produces a fine tone. More than that, though, and unlike a number of teenage wunderkind who have been foisted on the world in the recent years, Aldort doesn't just play the notes, he is clearly a musician and gave a musician's performance.We shall be hearing more from this young man."
Deryk Barker
Victoria Times Columnist

Naomi Aldort's youngest, Oliver Aldort, is a budding cellist and pianist performing solos with orchestras since the age of ten. You can visit Oliver at **www.OliverAldort.com**

Index